GETTING IT RIGHT

CHESS
AND
DRAUGHTS

GETTING IT RIGHT

CHESS AND DRAUGHTS

Albert Belasco

foulsham
LONDON • NEW YORK • TORONTO • SYDNEY

foulsham

Yeovil Road, Slough, Berkshire SL1 4JH

Typeset in Great Britain by Typesetting Solutions, Slough, Berks.
Printed in Great Britain by Cox & Wyman Ltd., Reading.

Contents

This little introduction to two of the most popular board games of all time will be all you need to help you to develop your game quickly and enjoyably. The emphasis throughout is on both of these qualities. You will also discover that two common fallacies are firmly dealt with, namely that chess is a difficult game and that draughts is an easy one!

They are, from one point of view, as easy or as difficult as the player will make them. However, these two fallacies can be stumbling blocks and this book is designed to take you safely over them.

Draughts is often assumed to be an inconsequential, light and easy game. For the beginner this is so, and is also the main reason why the game is suitable for people of all ages, from young to old. However, there is a lot more to it than this, as the section on draughts will demonstrate. This added depth to the game will open up new vistas of possibilities and enjoyment for the draughts player who intends to take the game seriously.

On the other hand, to the outsider, chess appears to be a fascinating but complicated and difficult game. Not so. Once the basic moves have been covered, it is possible to learn to play games that are intensely absorbing within a very short space of time. This, however, by no means changes the fact that chess is a game of infinite depth, complexity and possibilities. And you will begin to appreciate this right from the outset.

So, if you fancy your chances at winning chess or draughts, this book will help you to surprise your friends at your mental agility, gamesmanship and imaginative play. With your first game, whether of chess or draughts, you will be embarking on a course that will bring you endless stimulation and pleasure.

PART 1

DRAUGHTS

Chapter 1

INTRODUCTION

By way of an introduction to the game of draughts, the following is an extract from some correspondence which occurred in our daily papers, quite some number of years ago now. The statement that sparked off this controversy was to the effect that all possibilities regarding the game of draughts had been exhausted and that the reply to every possible move was known to those proficient in the game.

The response was sharp and to the point: 'I unequivocally deny that any recognized treatise on the game lays down the above absurd dictum. Indeed, the only work within my knowledge which contains this assertion is the *Encyclopaedia Britannica* (ninth edition), the draughts article in which was evidently written by a man who had no practical knowledge whatever of the game he so glibly stigmatised.

'I would ask, what is the experience of proficients? Do they not frequently see supposed draws, demonstrated as wins, and vice versa? Again, do they not also lose games in correspondence play, where they have every opportunity of ascertaining the correct reply by analysis?

'Further, can a game be considered as exhausted which furnishes weekly original matter sufficient to support dozens of draughts columns, not forgetting several voluminous monthly and quarterly publications?'

The language of this correspondence may seem now to be a little dated, but this is only the style. The message rings through as true and clear today as it did then. The possibilities, and therefore the enjoyment in this game, are almost limitless. Perhaps an adage for the prospective player to keep in mind is that everybody plays draughts, but the numbers of draughts players are very few indeed!

Chapter 2

THE LAWS OF DRAUGHTS

1 The Standard Board must be of light and dark squares, not less than fourteen and one-half inches (36.8 cm) or more than sixteen inches (40.6 cm) across said squares.

2. The Board shall be placed so that the bottom corner square on the left hand shall be black.

3. The Standard Men, technically described as Black and White, must be light and dark (say red and white, or black and white), turned, and round, and not less than one and one-eighth inch (2.86 cm) or more than one and one-quarter inch (3.18 cm) in diameter.

4. The men shall be placed on the black squares. (In all printed diagrams the white squares are used, for reasons which are obvious.)

5. The black men shall invariably be placed upon the real or supposed first twelve squares of the board; the white men upon the last twelve squares.

6. Each player shall play alternately with black and white men, and lots shall be cast for the colour only once — viz. at the commencement of a match — the winner to have the choice of taking either black or white.

7. The first move must invariably be made by the person having the black men.

8. At the end of five minutes (if the move has not been previously made) 'Time' must be called in a distinct manner by the person appointed for the purpose; and if the move be not completed on the expiry of another minute, the game shall be adjudged as lost through improper delay.

9. When there is only one way of taking one or more pieces, 'Time' shall be called at the end of one minute; if the move be not completed on the expiry of another minute, the game shall be adjudged as lost through improper delay.

10. Either player is entitled, on giving information, to arrange his own or opponent's pieces properly on the square. After the move has been made, however, if either player touch or arrange any piece without giving intimation to his opponent he shall be cautioned for the first offence, and shall forfeit the game for any subsequent act of the kind.

11. After the pieces have been arranged, if the person whose turn it is to play touch one, he must either play it or forfeit the game. When the piece is not playable he is penalised according to the preceding law.

12. If any part of a playable piece be played over an angle of the square on which it is stationed, the play must be completed in that direction.

13. A capturing play as well as an ordinary one is completed whenever the hand is withdrawn from the piece played, even though two or more pieces should have been taken.

14. When taken, if a player remove one of his own pieces, he cannot replace it; but his opponent can either play or insist on his replacing it.

15. Either player making a false or improper move shall instantly forfeit the game to his opponent, without another move being made.

16. The 'Huff' or 'Blow' is (before one plays his own piece) to remove from the board any one of the adverse pieces that might or should have been taken. But the Huff or Blow never constitutes play.

17. The player has the power either to Huff, compel the take, or to let the piece remain on the board, as he thinks proper.

18. When a Man first reaches any of the squares on the opposite extreme line of the board it becomes a King, and can be moved backwards or forwards, as the limits of the board permit (though not in the same play), and must be crowned (by placing a Man on the top of it) by the opponent; if he neglects to do so, and plays, any such play shall be put back until the Man be crowned.

19. A draw is when neither of the players can *force* a win. When one of the sides appears stronger than the other, the stronger party is required to complete the win, or to show to the satisfaction of the umpire or referee at least a decided advantage over his opponent within 40 of his own moves — to be counted from the point at which notice was given — failing in which, he must relinquish the game as a draw.

20. Anything which may tend either to annoy or distract the attention of the player is strictly forbidden — such as making signs or sounds, pointing or hovering over the board, unnecessarily delaying to move a piece touched, or smoking. Any principal so acting, after having been warned of the consequence, and requested to desist, shall forfeit the game.

21. While a game is pending, neither player is permitted to leave the room without sufficient reason, or receiving the other's consent or company.

22. Any spectator giving warning, either by sign, sound, or remark, on any of the games, whether played or pending, shall be ordered from the room during the match, and play will be discontinued until such offending party retires.

23. A match between equals, wins and draws to count, should consist of an even number of games, so that each player may have the first move the same number of times.

24. Either player committing a breach of any of these laws must submit to the penalty, and his opponent is equally bound to exact the same.

25. Should any dispute occur not satisfactorily determined by the preceding laws, a written statement of the facts must be sent to a disinterested arbiter having a knowledge of the game, whose decision shall be final.

Chapter 3

THE GAME OF DRAUGHTS

I t will probably surprise the student to learn that Draughts games may not only be recorded when played, but also carried on by correspondence; this feeling will in no wise be lessened when he or she discovers the extreme simplicity of the method employed, when being introduced to the numbered board.

THE NUMBERED BOARD

Figure 1

	1		2		3		4
5		6		7		8	
	9		10		11		12
13		14		15		16	
	17		18		19		20
21		22		23		24	
	25		26		27		28
29		30		31		32	

MEN AS PLACED AT THE COMMENCEMENT OF A GAME

Figure 2

Reference to the illustration reveals that the black occupy the squares numbered 1 to 12, and the white 21 to 32. Thus, when black, who always opens the game, moves out the third man from his single corner in the direction of his opponent's single corner, he will see how easy it is to record the fact that a man has been removed from square 11 to 15, possibly meeting with a reply of 22 to 18, and so on, until the conclusion of the game.

To illustrate this, and before proceeding further, number your board (as per the diagram on page 17), and play through the following game, the opening of which is appropriately termed the 'Single Corner', for the reason that the two first moves are made from one single corner to the other:

Played between Mr Bean and the Author — the latter's move.

Black	11	15	8	12	10	14	14	18
White	22	18	28	24	28	24	22	15
Black	15	22	16	20	3	7	13	17
White	25	18	32	28	11	8	21	7
Black	8	11	11	16	7	10	2	18
White	29	25	19	15	24	19	23	14
Black	4	8	10	19	9	13	16	32
White	25	22	24	15	18	9		
Black	12	16	7	10	5	14	Drawn	
White	24	19	15	11	8	4		

The order of play is shown by the line leading from the bottom of column 1 to the top of column 2, these two moves following each other, and so on until the last move at the end of column 4 is reached.

Assuming that you have now made yourself familiar with the 'language of the board', we will next proceed to a brief explanation of that which is of vital importance in playing the scientific game — *the theory of the move.*

Concerning the Move

The fact of having 'the move', and knowing how to utilise it, will in many positions enable one to draw, and even win games against a much superior opponent; and, as showing its importance, it may be noticed that in the majority of problematical endings it is the judicious handling of the move which brings about the desired result. There are several methods of discovering to whom the move belongs, but the most simple, and the only one to which we shall allude — it being quite adequate to meet all practical purposes — is the following:

Add together all the men (both your own and your adversary's) resting on the columns with a square at the bottom the colour of those upon which you are playing. If the number be an odd one, with your turn to play, you have the move: but if even, the move is with your opponent.

A careful study of the following diagram will fully illustrate the foregoing.

PROBLEM ILLUSTRATING THE MOVE

BLACK — *Moving Downward*

Figure 3

White to move and win

It will be seen that the combined number of the men on columns 1 and 3 is an odd one (3), thus, white has the move and wins by —

■ □

13	9	23	27	1	6	23	16	15	19
26	23	5	1	7	10	6	15	White	
9	5	27	23	15	19	16	20	wins	

Were it black's turn to play, he could, having the move, easily draw.

Should there be no men on columns 1, 2, 3 and 4, add up those on the columns with a square of the reverse colour at the bottom.

If you desire to alter the move you can invariably do so by an exchange of odd men, as 1 for 1, 3 for 3, etc.; but one of the *capturing* pieces must be removed from the board (The exchange in the solution to the problem above forcibly illustrates this, as both the kings making the capture remain on the board, and the move is not therefore changed.) or this rule will not apply. Even exchanges generally have no effect on the move.

The Positions

In connection with the Scientific Game there are four problematical situations which are known as the First, Second, Third and Fourth Positions. It is highly desirable that the student should make himself well acquainted with their many complications; and it has been said of the First Position, that no draughts player can truly call himself such until he has mastered it in all its interesting variations. A thorough knowledge of this Position will often prove apparent draws to be wins, and form the foundation of many an artistic finish.

FIRST POSITION

BLACK — *Moving Downward*

Figure 4

White to move and win

Solution

27 32	1-24 28	32 28	12 16	18 15	16 19	27 31	32 28
28 24	18 15	24 27	28 32	24 28	32 27	19 23	15 19
23 18	28 24	15 18	27 24	15 11	28 32	11 15	W.wins

Variation 1

12 16	15 18	19 16	23 19	8 11	27 23	3 8	White
18 15	24 19	18 23	11 8	32 27	8 3	18 15	wins
16 20	32 28	16 11	28 32	11 8	23 18	8 4	

In playing the variation, the student must branch off at the 3rd move (23   18) and, instead of replying with 24   28 (the move to which the figure 1 is attached), continue with the column headed *Var.* 1.

We give but one of many variations to this famous Position, as we consider the student will get most excellent practice by endeavouring to demonstrate the wins in other directions without assistance.

SECOND POSITION

BLACK — *Moving Downward*

Figure 5

Black to move and win

Solution

1	5	3	7	27	31	10	15	27	24	10	15	18	14
8	11	24	19	32	28	23	27	32	28	24	28	4	8
5	9	7	10	31	27	15	19	24	19	15	19	6	1
11	15	19	23	28	32	27	32	28	32	28	32	8	11
9	14	10	15	27	23	19	24	19	15	19	24	14	9
15	11	23	27	32	28	32	28	32	28	32	28	13	6
14	18	15	19	23	18	24	27	15	10	11	16	1	10
11	16	27	32	28	24	28	24	28	24	28	19	11	16
18	15	19	24	18	14	27	32	10	6	16	23	10	15
16	20	32	28	24	19	24	28	24	19	12	8	16	20
15	11	24	27	6	10	32	27	14	10	23	18	15	19
20	24	28	32	19	23	28	32	10	24	8	4	B. wins	

THIRD POSITION

BLACK

Figure 6

WHITE

Black to move and win

Solution

13	9	18	15	22	26	10	14	7	11	26	22	12	8
22	18	1	6	14	18	31	27	22	25	24	20	26	22
9	6	14	17	5	9	18	22	11	15	22	26	8	3
18	22	6	2	10	6	27	23	25	22	20	16	14	9
6	1	17	14	9	13	22	25	23	27	26	22	15	10
22	18	25	22	6	10	2	7	22	2	16	12	Black
21	25	15	10	26	31	25	22	27	24	22	26	wins

Very critical, and requires extreme care in forcing the win.

FOURTH POSITION

Black man on 21; Kings on 22, 23, 28. White man on 30; Kings on 31, 32.

Solution of Black to move and win

28	24	28	32	23	19	32	27	18	22	22	26	28	24
32	28	22	18	27	31	24	28	31	27	30	23	B.	wins
24	20	31	27	19	24	27	32						

Solution of White to move and draw

31	27	27	31	32	27	27	32	31	27	27	31	31	26
23	19	19	24	24	20	22	18	28	24	18	23	Drawn	

Openings of Games

There are about forty classified Openings; we will, however, content ourselves by giving twenty of the most popular.

We offer no opinion as to the merits of any particular line of play, but would strongly advise the student to select, say, four Openings from the list appended and practise them whenever an opportunity presents itself. He or she will thus gradually become so familiar with their variations as to make quite a formidable stand when meeting an opponent on what we might term as their favourite battle-grounds.

The moves following the title of the game define the opening.

				Black	
'Double Corner'	.....	.....	.....	.....	9 14
'Edinburgh'	.....	.....	.....	.....	9 13
'Dundee'	.....	.....	.....	.....	12 16

■ □

					Black	
'Denny'	.....	.....	.....	.....	10	14
'Kelso'	.....	.....	.....	.....	10	15

				Black		White	
'Switcher'	.....	.....	.....	11	15	21	17
'Single Corner'	.....	.....	.....	11	15	22	18
'Cross'	.....	.....	.....	11	15	23	18
'Paisley'	.....	.....	.....	11	16	24	19

			Black		White		Black	
'Ayrshire Lassie'	.....	.....	11	15	24	20	9	11
'Bristol'	.....	.....	11	16	24	20	16	19
'Will-o'-the-Wisp'	.....	.....	11	15	23	19	9	13
'Dyke'	.....	.....	11	15	22	17	15	19

	Black		White		Black		White		Black	
'Whilter'	11	15	23	19	9	14	22	17	7	11
'Souter'	11	15	23	19	9	14	22	17	6	9
'Glasgow'	11	15	23	19	8	11	22	17	11	16
'Maid o' the Mill'	11	15	22	17	8	11	17	13	15	18
'Fife'	11	15	23	19	9	14	22	17	5	9
'Laird and Lady'	11	15	23	19	8	11	22	17	9	13
'Old 14th'	11	15	23	19	8	11	22	17	4	8

NB — This latter opening (the Old 14th) is so called by reason of the fact that it was the fourteenth game in Sturges' famous work, published in 1800. Many of the preceding Openings were, however, named by Wyllie, the late World Champion.

In Club and Match play, the modern practice is to ballot for openings restricted to first move on either side, which much widens the field of play.

■ □

Early Losses

'BRISTOL'

11 16	16 20	A-8 11	10 19	9 18	4 11
23 18	24 19	19 15	18 14	22 8	27 24
					W. wins

A — The earliest recorded loss. It was published at Saragossa in 1650 by Don Juan Garcia Canalajas in a work entitled *Libro Del Jeugo de la Damas.*

'AYRSHIRE LASSIE'

11 15	8 11	9 13	A-4 8	11 20	White
24 20	28 24	23 19	20 16	22 17	wins
		A — Forming Trap			

'SINGLE CORNER'

In connection with this game, Black can often lay a very neat trap, humorously named the 'Goose Walk'. The play leading up to it is as follows:

11 15	8 11	12 16	15 19	9 14	5 14
22 18	29 25	24 20	24 15	18 9	Black
15 22	4 8	10 15	16 19	11 25	wins
25 18	25 22	*27 24	23 16	28 24	

*Both 27 24 and 28 24 lose here.

Black must not king the man on 25 until 31 or 26 has been moved, thus preventing an exchange.

'CROSS'

11 15	23 19	15 18	24 15	10 19	32 27
23 18	9 14	26 22	11 18	17 10	16 20
8 11	18 9	18 23	22 15	6 15	30 26
27 23	5 14	19 15	A-7 10	27 4	White
4 8	22 17	10 19	31 27	12 16	wins
		A — Forming Trap			

'EDINBURGH'

9	13	24	15	11	16	A-26	22	16	23	18	14
22	18	11	18	26	23	4	8	27	18	8	11
10	15	28	24	6	9	22	15	7	10	Black
18	14	8	11	31	26	9	18	14	7	wins
15	19	23	19	1	6	23	14	3	28	

A — Forms Trap

Interesting Games

We would remind the student that Black moves first.

'SINGLE CORNER'

The following is one of four games played by Correspondence between J. H. Strudwick (London) and J. A. Kear (Bristol). The former's move. The result was one win each, and two drawn.

11	15	12	16	10	15	9	14	A-2	6	22	18
22	18	24	19	18	11	19	16	27	24	13	22
15	22	16	20	8	24	4	8	20	27	18	2
25	18	26	22	28	19	23	19	32	23	Black
9	13	5	9	6	10	8	11	11	20	resigns
29	25	21	17	25	21	30	26		

A — Losing move.

'EDINBURGH CROSS'

Played between R. Atwell and A. Jordan. The latter's move. One of the shortest games on record, in which Atwell certainly caught the ex-Champion of England 'dozing'.

9	13	24	20	5	9	25	21	24	19	32	28
23	18	6	10	21	17	2	6	15	24	W. wins
10	15	28	24	1	5				

■ □

'WHITE DYKE'

The following is one of four wins scored for Dunedin, New Zealand, in a match with Christchurch.

11	15	15	18	9	13	12	26	1	17	26	23
22	17	24	19	30	26	31	15	13	29	2	6
8	11	11	16	6	9	14	18	15	10	23	32
17	14	25	21	26	22	24	19	29	25	6	10
9	18	16	20	7	11	5	9	10	6	8	11
23	14	29	25	22	15	10	6	25	22	15	8
10	17	6	9	11	18	9	14	19	15	3	12
21	14	28	24	14	10	6	1	22	26	Black	
4	8	1	6	9	14	2	6	6	2	wins	
26	23	32	28	19	16						

'CROSS'

Played between E. Sutherst (London) and T. Goldsboro (Bradford). The former's move. A recent illustration of a neat 'stroke' finish.

11	15	18	9	11	18	28	24	16	20	30	26
23	18	5	14	22	15	2	7	21	17	23	30
8	11	22	17	10	19	24	19	11	16	32	7
27	23	15	18	24	15	11	16	10	7	30	14
4	8	26	22	14	18	17	14	3	10	7	2
23	19	18	23	31	27	A-7	11	27	24	16	23
9	14	19	15	7	11	14	10	20	27	2	27
										W. wins	

A — 7 10 draws. The 'stroke' appears to be forced from here. — T.G.

'DOUBLE CORNER'

The following is known as 'Wyllie's Early Stroke'.

9	14	15	19	12	19	5	9	9	14	15	22
22	17	24	15	17	10	17	13	26	23	25	2
11	15	10	19	6	15	2	6	19	26	White	
25	22	23	16	21	17	30	25	22	18	wins	

'DOUBLE CORNER DYKE'

One of 28 Simultaneous Blindfold Games contested by
Willie Gardner, Blindfold Champion of the World. In
evidence of the fact that this remarkable player 'saw'
exactly what he was doing, we may mention the following: During one of his Blindfold displays, a slight confusion was caused by one of his opponents, as the games
were drawing to a close. At the request of the Champion
the men were replaced on each board; and then, to the
astonishment of all present, *he proceeded to call out the
moves on each side to the point where the difficulty had arisen.*

9 14	4 8	16 20	30 26	11 18	23 19
22 17	22 17	26 22	2 7	31 26	11 15
11 15	15 18	7 11	26 22	12 16	28 24
25 22	24 19	22 15	7 11	19 12	5 9
8 11	11 16	11 18	22 15	8 11	26 22
17 13	29 25				

And White, the Champion, wins.

'BRISTOL'

Played between J. Wyllie, late Champion of the World,
and H. Hamilton, of Glasgow. The former's move.

11 16	2 7	6 10	11 16	16 23	3 10
22 18	27 24	15 6	28 24	27 11	23 18
10 14	16 20	1 10	8 11	20 27	16 20
24 19	31 27	21 17	6 2	32 23	18 11
7 10	4 8	14 21	7 10	10 15	10 15
25 22	19 15	18 14	2 6	25 22	30 25
8 11	10 19	9 18	11 15	12 16	21 30
29 25	24 15	22 6	23 19	11 7	6 10

W. wins

One of the rare occasions on which the World's Champion 'went down'.

'OLD FOURTEENTH'

Played in Dunedin between Mr. D. A. Brodie (blind-fold) and Mr. P. McKenzie. The latter's move.

11	15	4	8	9	14	6	15	16	23	18	25
23	19	17	13	26	23	28	24	20	16	27	4
8	11	15	18	10	15	12	16	11	20	W. wins	
22	17	24	20	A-19	10	23	19	25	22		

A — The winning move.

'CROSS'

Played between A. Bell and the Author. The former's move.

11	15	22	8	11	15	22	18	6	9	23	16
23	18	4	11	32	28	15	22	18	15	12	19
8	11	28	19	15	24	26	10	3	8	10	6
18	14	5	9	28	19	7	14	30	25	19	24
10	17	25	21	2	7	31	26	8	12	6	1
21	14	9	14	27	23	1	6	25	22	24	27
9	18	29	25	10	15	26	22	9	13	1	6
24	19	7	10	19	10	12	16	15	10	27	31
15	24	25	22	6	15	22	18	16	19	6	9
										W. wins	

Draughts Problems

For Solutions to the following, see page 37.

■ □

No. 1. BY W. G. W. LEGGETT, LONDON

BLACK

Figure 7

WHITE

Black to play and win

No. 2. BY THE AUTHOR

BLACK

Figure 8

WHITE

White to play and win

◼ ☐

No. 3. BY JAMES WYLLIE, DUNDEE (late World Champion)

BLACK

Figure 9

WHITE

White to play and win

No. 4. BY JOSHUA STURGES

BLACK

Figure 10

WHITE

White to play and win

33

No. 5. BY G. H. SLOCUM, USA

BLACK

Figure 11

WHITE

White to play and win

No. 6. BY W. PAYNE, LONDON (1756)

BLACK

Figure 12

WHITE

White to play and win. Useful to the novice.

No. 7. BY FRANK DUNNE, WARRINGTON

BLACK

Figure 13

WHITE

Black to play, white to win.

No. 8. BY A. JORDAN, LONDON

BLACK

Figure 14

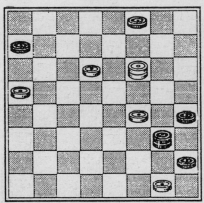

WHITE

White to play and win.

35

■ □

No. 9. BY W. D. BENSTEAD, LOWESTOFT

BLACK

Figure 15

WHITE

White to play and win.

No. 10. BY C. F. BARKER, USA

BLACK

Figure 16

WHITE

White to play and win.

■ □

No. 11. BY H. D. LYMAN, USA

BLACK

Figure 17

WHITE

Black to play and win.

Solutions to Draughts Problems

No. 1 — By W. G. W. Leggett. Black wins by:

28	24	9	6	14	18	2	7	3	8	4	11
13	9	10	15	6	2	23	27	11	18	23	16
24	19	7	10	18	23	7	11	19	23		

No. 2 — By the Author. White wins by:

A-26	22	13	6	5	1	18	25	1	19

A — 5 1 draws, and 9 6 loses for White.

No. 3 — By James Wyllie. White wins by:

26	30	11	7	18	14	10	7	6	22	30	7	7	10
28	19	2	11	9	18	3	10	17	26	13	17		

37

No. 4 — By Joshua Sturges. White wins as follows:

32 27	28 32	27 24	19 28	26 23

No. 5 — By G. H. Slocum. White wins as follows:

6 1	11 15	1 5	19 23	13 15	15 24
8 11	7 10	9 13	5 9	16 19	28 17
3 7	15 19	12 16			

No. 6 — By W. Payne. White wins as follows:

18 15	14 9	23 19	9 6	19 24	24 19
A– 6 1	24 28	1 5	28 32	5 1	
—24 28, 23	27, 6 1, 14	10, 28 32, 27	24, 1 5, 10 6.		

No. 7 — By Frank Dunne. White wins as follows:

11 16	16 11	11 4	4 8	8 12	12 8	7 11
18 23	12 8	19 15	23 18	18 14	14 9	9 14

No. 8 — By A. Jordan. White wins as follows:

11 15	19 16	16 11	11 7	7 2	13 9	15 19
3 8	8 12	12 16	16 19	19 23	5 14	24 6

No. 9 — By W. D. Benstead. White wins as follows:

25 22	21 17	22 25	31 26	26 17
10 15	30 26	26 30	30 14	

No. 10 — By C. F. Barker. White wins as follows:

15 10	7 14	22 17	14 21	26 23

No. 11 — By H. D. Lyman. Black wins as follows:

14 17	21 14	8 3	7 11	6 10

PART 2

CHESS

Chapter 4

INTRODUCTION

◼▬▬▬▬ ▬▬▬▬◻

Description of the Chess Board and Men — Arrangement of the Men — The King — The Queen — The Rooks and Castles — The Bishops — The Knights — The Pawns — Their Movements, Powers and Methods of Capture.

The game of Chess, perhaps the most fascinating pastime which the 'wisdom of antiquity' has bequeathed to us, is played by two people, each having at their command a little army of sixteen men, on a board divided into 64 squares, eight on each of four sides. The squares are usually coloured white and black, or red and white, alternately; custom has made it a regulation that the board shall be so placed that each player has a white square at his or her right-hand corner.

This arrangement is merely conventional. In the earlier ages of chess, the board was simply divided into 64 squares, without any difference of colour; there is good reason for believing that the chessmen were then alike in form and size, and distinguishable only by an inscription or sign on each one.

Modern chess has entered popular awareness and culture mainly through the publicity it receives when world championships are reviewed, some world champions even achieving the status of household names. Capablanca and Alekhine were two former world champions (and great rivals), but it was Steinitz, an earlier champion, who has probably contributed most to chess theory.

The modern era has been dominated by the Russians, with Karpov and Kasparov its present-day stars. Many people will know the name of Bobby Fischer, the American whose name was synonymous with chess.

Matches and tournaments are usually decided using a points system, commonly one point for a win and half a point for a draw. A time limit is normally imposed on the number of moves each player can make in a prescribed period and 20 to 24 moves an hour is appropriate. A player who overruns the time limit is deemed to have forfeited the game.

A chess clock is used to record the time taken by each player. This consists of two ordinary clocks connected by a lever which, when depressed, stops the clock on the one side and restarts it on the other. When you have made your move you press your lever, thus stopping your clock and starting your opponent's.

The Fédération Internationale des Echecs (FIDE) is the recognised world body responsible for the World Championship and Chess Olympiad arrangements. Grandmaster and International Master titles are conferred by the FIDE from time to time on players whose performance in international events has reached the required standard. Titles below this level, such as National Master and Candidate Master, are awarded by national chess authorities. Many countries now also grade players with a recognized rating derived from their performances over a period in approved matches and tournaments.

Although fashions change in the style in which chess is played, the underlying principles remain constant and so it is with a good grounding in the classical approach that a start will here be made.

The following diagram represents the board with all the men arranged in proper order for the commencement of a game:

BLACK

Figure 18

WHITE

Each player, it will be observed, has eight superior pieces or officers, and eight minor ones, which are called Pawns; and for the purpose of distinction, the Pieces and Pawns of one party are of a different colour to those of the other.

The eight superior Pieces, on each side, are:

A King . . . . ♚

A Queen . . . . ♛

Two Rooks, or Castles . . . . ♜
   (as they are indiscriminately called)
Two Bishops . . . . ♝

Two Knights . . . . ♞

And each of these Pieces has his Pawn
   or Foot-soldier . . . . ♟

making in all an array of sixteen men on each side.

On beginning a game, these Pieces and Pawns are disposed in the manner shown on the foregoing diagram. The King and Queen occupy the centre squares of the first or 'royal' line, as it is called, and each has for its supporters a Bishop, a Knight, and a Rook, while before the whole stand the Pawns or Foot-soldiers in a row. (To prevent a common error among young players, of misplacing the King and Queen on commencing a game, it is well to bear in mind that at the outset each Queen should stand on a square of her own colour.) The Pieces on the King's side of the board are called the King's, as (moving in order of placement away from the King)

44

King's Bishop, King's Knight, King's Rook; and the Pawns directly in front of them, the King's Pawn, King's Bishop's Pawn, King's Knight's Pawn, and King's Rook's Pawn. The Pieces on the Queen's side are, in like manner, called the Queen's Bishop, Queen's Knight and Queen's Rook; and the Pawns before them, Queen's Pawn, Queen's Bishop's Pawn, Queen's Knight's Pawn, and Queen's Rook's Pawn.

Movement of the Pieces and Pawns

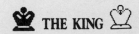 THE KING

The King can move one square only at a time (except in 'Castling' which will be explained later), but he can make this move in any direction, forwards, backwards, laterally or diagonally. The original movement of the King, or 'Rey' as he was first called in Europe, appears to have been very limited, since he was restricted from moving at all, except by the necessity of extricating himself from an adverse check. About the beginning of the thirteenth century, he had the power of playing one square directly, but was not permitted to move or capture angularly; this limitation, however, lasted for only a short period, and then the Rey had the privilege of moving and taking in any direction, as at present, but his range of action never extended beyond one square. He can take any one of the adversary's men which stands on an adjoining square to that he occupies, provided such man is left unprotected, and he has the peculiar

45

privilege of being himself exempt from capture. He is not permitted, however, to move into check, that is, on to any square which is guarded by a Piece or Pawn of the enemy, nor can he, under any circumstance, be played to an adjacent square to that on which the rival King is stationed. Like most of the other Pieces, his power is greatest in the middle of the board, where, without obstruction, he has the choice of eight different squares. At the sides, he may play to any one of five, but when in the angles of the board, three squares only are at his command.

♛ THE QUEEN ♕

The Queen is by far the most powerful of the forces. She has the advantage of moving as a Rook, in straight lines, forwards, backwards, and sideways to the extent of the board in all directions, and as a Bishop, diagonally, with the same range. To comprehend her scope of action, place her alone in the centre of the board; it will then be seen that she has command of no less than twenty-seven squares, besides the one she stands on. (See Figure 21).

♜ THE ROOK ♖

The Rook or Castle, is next in power to the Queen. He moves in a straight line, forwards, backwards, or sideways, having a uniform range, on a clear board, of fourteen squares, exclusive of the one he occupies. (See 'Castling', page 67.)

♟ THE BISHOP ♗

The Bishop moves diagonally forwards or backwards, to the extent of the board. It follows, therefore, that he travels throughout the game only on squares of the same colour as the one on which he stands when the game begins and that each player has a Bishop running on white squares, and one on black squares. When placed on a centre square of a clear board, he will be found to have a range of thirteen squares.

♞ THE KNIGHT ♘

The action of the Knight is peculiar, and not easy to describe. He is the only one of the Pieces which has the privilege of leaping over another man. The movements of the others are all dependent on their freedom from obstruction by their own and the enemy's men. For example, when the forces are duly ranged in order of battle before the commencement of the game, the Knight is the only one of the eight capital Pieces which can be played before the Pawns are moved — King, Queen, Bishop, and Rook are all hemmed in by the rank of Pawns, which they cannot overleap; but the Knight, having the liberty of springing over the heads of other men, can be brought into the field at once. In this case, as his move is one square *in a straight line,* and *one in an oblique direction,* if the King's Knight were to begin the game, he must be played either to King's Rook's third square, or to King's Bishop's third square; and if the

Queen's Knight commenced, he must be moved to Queen's Rook's third square, or to Queen's Bishop's third square.

The following diagram will serve, perhaps, to make his action better understood. (See also pages 53 and 93 for a description of the powers and peculiarities of this Piece).

BLACK

Figure 19

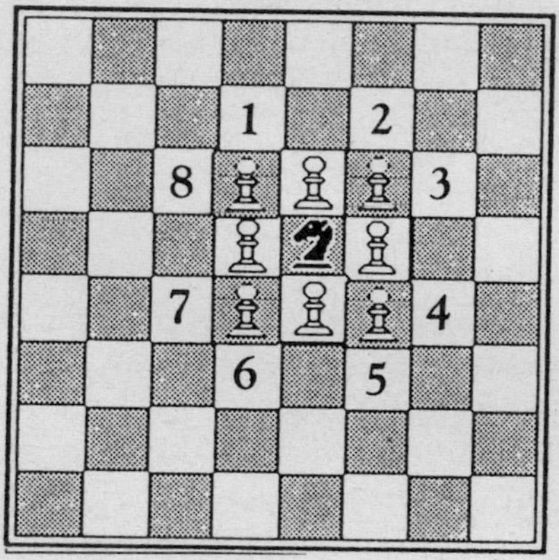

WHITE

In this position we have the Knight surrounded by Pawns in a way which would render any other Piece immovable. A King, Queen, Rook, or Bishop, so encompassed by their own forces, could never stir until one of the men were moved to make an outlet; and, if thus shut in by *adverse* Pawns, could escape only by being enabled to capture one or other of them. But the Knight clears such impediments at a bound, and can here be played to any one of the eight white squares around. It is worth remarking, that if he is stationed on a *white* square in the centre of the board, he has then eight *black* squares at this choice; because, from the peculiarity of his move, it is impossible for him to spring from one white square to another white one, or from a black square to a black square. On placing him on any square at the side of the board, it will be seen that his scope of action is much diminished, and when standing on either of the four corners, or Rook's squares, as they are called, he has then only two squares to which he can leap.

♟ THE PAWN ♙

The Pawn moves only one square at a time, and that *straight forward,* except in the act of capturing, when it takes one step diagonally to the right or left file on to the square occupied by the man taken, and continues on that file until it captures another man. A power has been conceded to it, however, in latter times, of going *two steps when first played* in the game, *provided no hostile Pawn commands the first square over which he moves,* but, in that case, the adverse Pawn has the option of taking him in his passage, *as if he had moved one step only* (see Figure 26). A Pawn is the only one of the forces *which goes out of his direction to capture,* and which has not the advantage of moving backwards; but it has one remarkable privilege, by which on occasions it becomes invaluable, *whenever it reaches the extreme square of the file on which it travels, it is invested with the title and assumes the power of any superior*

Piece, except the King, which the player chooses. From this circumstance it frequently happens that one party, by skilful management of his Pawns, contrives to have two, and sometimes even three, Queens on the board at once, a combination of force which of course is irresistible.

On Capturing an Adverse Man

The 'Pieces' by which title the eight superior officers are technically designated, in contradistinction to the 'Pawns', all take in the same direction in which they move. This act consists in removing the adverse Piece or Pawn from the board, and placing the captor on the square the former occupied. To make this clear, we will begin with the King, and show his mode of capturing an adverse man.

BLACK

Figure 20

WHITE

Supposing the above to be the position of the men towards the conclusion of a game, and it being either party's turn to play, he could take the adverse Pawn from the board, and place his King on the square it occupied; and by doing so, the King would not depart from the order of his march, which, as we have before said, permits him to move *one step* in every direction. In each of these instances we have placed the Pawn in *front* of the King, but he would be equally entitled to take it were it standing on any other of the eight squares immediately surrounding him, *always provided it was not sustained or guarded by some other Piece or Pawn.*

The next diagram will exhibit the power of the Queen in capturing an enemy.

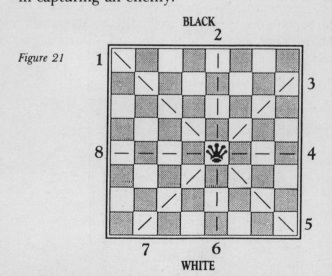

Figure 21

Thus placed in the middle of the board, the range of

the Queen is immense. She has here the option of taking any one of eight men if they were placed at the extremities of the board, on the squares respectively numbered 1, 2, 3, 4, 5, 6, 7, and 8, should her line of march be unobstructed; and if these men were nearer, on any of the intermediate squares, indicated by the dotted lines, she would be equally enabled to take any one of them at her choice. Like all the other Pieces and Pawns she effects the capture by removing the man from the board, and stationing herself on the vacated square.

The *Rook* has the same power in taking as the Queen, forwards, backwards and sideways, but he cannot, like her, take any man diagonally.

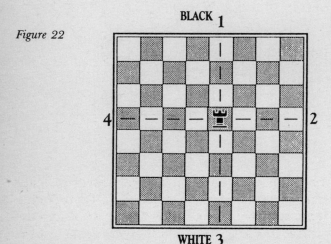

Figure 22

BLACK 1

WHITE 3

For example, place the Rook in the centre of the board, and an opposing man on each of the squares numbered, and the Rook has the power of taking any one of the four; he has the same power if the Pieces are on any of the intervening squares as indicated.

The *Bishop* takes, as he moves, diagonally, either forwards or backwards, his range extending, on unobstructed squares, to the extent of the diagonal line on which he travels.

Figure 23

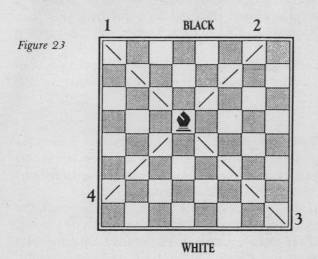

The *Knight*, as we have seen before, moves or leaps one square forward and one obliquely, his action being a combination of the shortest move of the Rook and the shortest move of the Bishop. In other words, he moves to the next square but one — of a different colour. His power and method of taking an opponent's man will be seen from Figure 24.

BLACK

Figure 24

WHITE

In this situation, in the centre of the board, he would have the power of taking any one of the men stationed on the squares numbered, by removing the man and placing himself on the vacant square.

There is no evidence, we believe, to show that the Knight has undergone any variation in action or power, since the first introduction of chess into Europe. His move appears to be supplementary to the range of the other forces, and to comprehend just those squares of the board over which none of them, similarly placed, would have command.

The *Pawn,* as we have previously observed, is the only man which captures in a direction different from his line of march. He is permitted to move only one square forward at a time, except on his first move, and is not allowed to take any Piece or Pawn which may impede his path. If, however, he meets with any of the adverse force on a point diagonal, one step either to the right or left of the square he occupies, he is at liberty to capture that man and take his place on the next file; for example:

BLACK

Figure 25

WHITE

Suppose, at the opening of the game, White begins by playing P-K4 (see the description of Notation, page 59), Black may reply in the same manner with P-K4, and neither Pawn can do more than remain an obstruction to the onward march of the other. But if Black instead played P-Q4 as in Figure 25, then White, if he likes, may take the adverse Pawn from the board and place his own in its stead. To exemplify another peculiarity of the Pawn, suppose White in this situation preferred playing the Pawn on to K5, instead of taking Black's Pawn, the following would be the situation:

BLACK

Figure 26

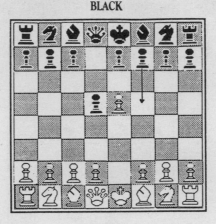

WHITE

If, now, Black chose to play P-KB4 as shown by the arrow, White has the option of taking that Pawn (in passing, as it is called), just as if Black, instead of playing it two steps had moved it to KB3 only. White, in fact, might arrest it in its leap over the King's Bishop's third square, take it off the board, and station his King's Pawn on the said Bishop's third square, as in an ordinary case of capture. But if he omit to exercise this power at once, he is not allowed to do so after another move has been made.

The reason for this power of taking *en passant* will be readily understood when it is remembered that formerly Pawns were only allowed to move one square at a time. To accelerate the opening of a game Pawns were given the privilege of either moving one or two squares on the first move, at the will of the player. This privilege, however, does not override the much older *right* of an

56

opposing Pawn to capture as if the Pawn had only been played one square; hence the *en passant* rule.

This privilege of the Pawn to take, in passing, another Pawn which attempts to advance two steps when first moved, is often imperfectly understood by beginners, and is the cause of so much misunderstanding, that every one should comprehend it thoroughly before beginning to play a game in earnest.

Chapter 5

CHESS NOTATION

I t will be obvious that without any easy method of recording games, chess players would not only be precluded from studying the games and analysis of their contemporaries, but would also be shut out from the great quantity of chess literature that centuries of skill and industry have accumulated. Notation is, in short, the language of the game, and it has taken many years to evolve the present simple form of recording games. Various systems have from time to time been tried. But here — this not purporting to be a history of notation — we shall but briefly mention two, which will suffice for all practical purposes for the student.

The *English Notation* or 'descriptive notation', adaptations of which are used in various countries, is based on naming each file from the piece that stands on it at the beginning of the game, and numbering the eight squares of the file from one to eight from each side of the board, as in the following diagram:

Figure 27

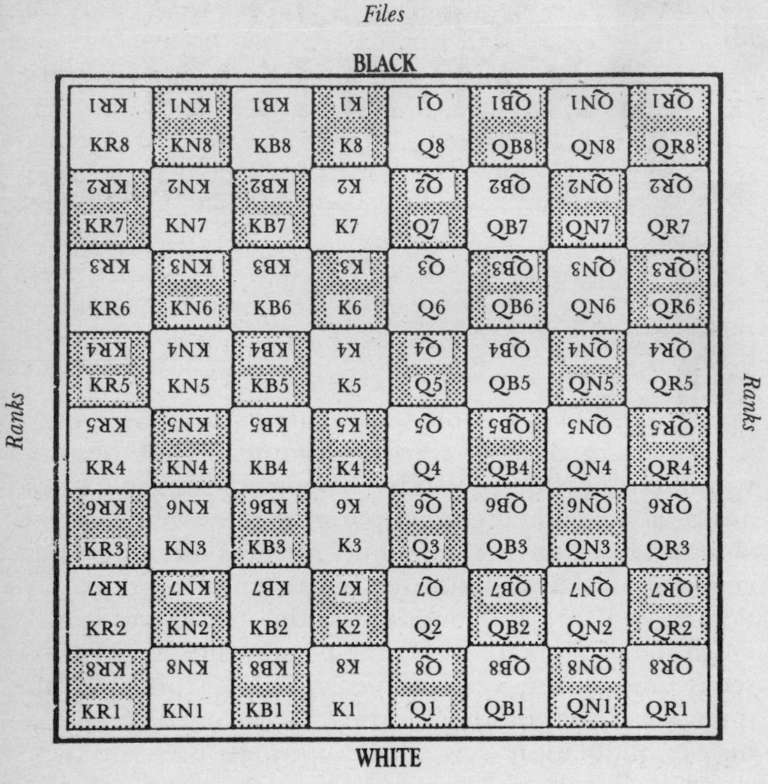

Files

BLACK

KR	KN	KB	K	Q	QB	QN	QR
KR1 / KR8	KN1 / KN8	KB1 / KB8	K1 / K8	Q1 / Q8	QB1 / QB8	QN1 / QN8	QR1 / QR8
KR2 / KR7	KN2 / KN7	KB2 / KB7	K2 / K7	Q2 / Q7	QB2 / QB7	QN2 / QN7	QR2 / QR7
KR3 / KR6	KN3 / KN6	KB3 / KB6	K3 / K6	Q3 / Q6	QB3 / QB6	QN3 / QN6	QR3 / QR6
KR4 / KR5	KN4 / KN5	KB4 / KB5	K4 / K5	Q4 / Q5	QB4 / QB5	QN4 / QN5	QR4 / QR5
KR5 / KR4	KN5 / KN4	KB5 / KB4	K5 / K4	Q5 / Q4	QB5 / QB4	QN5 / QN4	QR5 / QR4
KR6 / KR3	KN6 / KN3	KB6 / KB3	K6 / K3	Q6 / Q3	QB6 / QB3	QN6 / QN3	QR6 / QR3
KR7 / KR2	KN7 / KN2	KB7 / KB2	K7 / K2	Q7 / Q2	QB7 / QB2	QN7 / QN2	QR7 / QR2
KR8 / KR1	KN8 / KN1	KB8 / KB1	K8 / K1	Q8 / Q1	QB8 / QB1	QN8 / QN1	QR8 / QR1

Ranks ... Ranks

WHITE

Files

It will be seen that the files have the same name for each player, but the numbers are different. Thus White's King's Bishop's Square, or K B 1 as it is concisely written, is Black's King's Bishop's Eighth, or K B 8. White's K 3 is Black's K 6, etc. It may be thought that this double numbering would lead to confusion, but it rarely does; and very little practice will enable the student to visualise any square on the board.

Note that, to avoid confusion with 'K' for King, the Knight is abbreviated to 'N'.

The Pawns are named after the Piece in front of which each stands. That in front of the King is the King's Pawn, K P; that in front of the Queen's Rook is the Queen's Rook's Pawn, or Q R P, etc.

Having now a separate name for each square on the board, moves are recorded by naming the Piece to be moved and the square to which it is played. The first three moves of the Ruy Lopez opening would be written as follows:

WHITE	BLACK
1 King's Pawn to King's Fourth Square.	1 King's Pawn to King's Fourth Square.
2 King's Knight to King's Bishop's Third Square.	2 Queen's Knight to Queen's Bishop's Third Square.
3 King's Bishop to Queen's Knight's Fifth Square.	3 King's Knight to King's Bishop's Third Square.

This is the notation fully written, and as it is to be found in the old books. It was seen that all this is unnecessary, so it was contracted thus:

WHITE	BLACK
1 K P to K 4th	1 K P to K 4th
2 K N to K B 3rd	2 Q N to Q B 3rd
3 K B to Q N 5th	3 K N to K B 3rd

As in the vast majority of cases only one Piece or Pawn can be played to the same square, it is therefore

unnecessary to state the particular Piece or Pawn, *i.e.*
King's Bishop or Queen's Bishop. By substituting a
dash — for the word 'to' the English notation, as
generally written, becomes:

WHITE	BLACK
1 P — K 4	1 P — K 4
2 N — K B 3	2 N — Q B 3
3 B — N 5	3 N — B 3

Occasionally the dash is omitted and the move simply written, P K 4; but the dash, by distinguishing the
Piece from the square, is an assistance to the student.

It will be observed that with regard to the first move,
since only one Pawn can be played to K 4, it is
unnecessary to say King's Pawn, so the K is omitted.
With regard to the second move, each Knight could be
played to its Bishop's Third, hence K or Q, according as
it is the King's or Queen's Knight is moved, must be
added. Sometimes this move would be written K N —
B 3 instead of K N — K B 3, but the latter is perhaps
more consistent.

In the above example White's third move is written
simply B — N 5: had his Queen's Pawn been previously
played to Q 4, so that either of his Bishops could move
to N 5 (the *King's* Bishop to *Queen's* Knight 5 or the
Queen's Bishop to *King's* Knight 5), it would have been
necessary to show which Bishop he intended to move.
The move actually taken would be then recorded B —
Q N 5 or K B — N 5 — preferably the former. It will be
noticed that at his third move, Black, having already
played one N to B 3, only one can now be played there,
so it is merely stated N – B 3.

If a piece is to be taken, the multiplication sign × is used, as B × N, P × P, etc. When check is written, ch. is written after the move, thus, B — N 5 ch., R × P ch., etc. If double check is given (*i.e.* check by two or more pieces), db. is inserted before the ch., as N — B-4 db. ch. Sometimes the sign + denotes check, but as this sign is used in the analysis of the present work to show when either side has a superiority, its double use was not thought advisable. Discovered check is shown — d. ch.

When this notation was first introduced, one would come across such legends as the following, in the middle of a game, to denote a simple move.

King's Bishop's Pawn takes King's Knight's Pawn.

With initials only this reads:

K B P × K N P

It is, however, only in extremely rare cases, that all this is essential. The rare case is — when *both* of Black's Knight's Pawns can be taken, and both can be taken withal, by *either of two Pawns of White*. Ordinarily,. P × P would be sufficient, but if more than one Pawn can take, and more than one Pawn can be taken, the exact Pawns concerned must then be indicated. The rule therefore for modern English notation, is to give what is essential to describe the move, and *no more*. It sometimes happens that two Pieces can take the same Piece or Pawn, or move to the same square. The square on which the Piece stands that is to be moved is then placed in brackets, thus:

N (K 4) × B

This means that either of White's Knights could take a Black Bishop, and he does so with the one on K 4.

The *German Notation* is founded on numbering and lettering the board as in the following diagram:

Figure 28

BLACK

a8	b8	c8	d8	e8	f8	g8	h8
a7	b7	c7	d7	e7	f7	g7	h7
a6	b6	c6	d6	e6	f6	g6	h6
a5	b5	c5	d5	e5	f5	g5	h5
a4	b4	c4	d4	e4	f4	g4	h4
a3	b3	c3	d3	e3	f3	g3	h3
a2	b2	c2	d2	e2	f2	g2	h2
a1	b1	c1	d1	e1	f1	g1	h1

WHITE

The moves are shown by giving the squares on which the Piece stands, and the one to which it is to be moved. In the case of the Pawns the squares merely are given, but with Pieces the initial letter of the Piece (in capitals) is also given, though this is not essential. The first few moves in the Giucco Piano Opening read thus in the German notation:

1	*e* 2 — *e* 4	*e* 7 — *e* 5
2	S *g* 1 — *f* 3	S *b* 8 — *c* 6
3	L *f* 1 — *c* 4	L *f* 8 — *c* 5
4	*d* 2 — *d* 3	*d* 7 — *d* 6

■ □

At first this form of naming the squares is puzzling. With a little practice, however, they become as easy to locate as in the English system, possibly easier, since neither ranks nor files are duplicated. It is more consistently concise too, for since no two Pieces can stand on the same square at the same time, naming the square which a Piece leaves as well as that to which it goes, precludes all possibility of misunderstanding. In this system × means takes; + check; † takes with a check; ‡ mate.

Both the English and the German systems of notation are commonly used in fractional form, the moves of the White Pieces being recorded above the line, and Black below, as follows:

1 $\dfrac{\text{P} - \text{K}\,4}{\text{P} - \text{K}\,4}$ 2 $\dfrac{\text{N} - \text{K}\,\text{B}\,3}{\text{N} - \text{Q}\,\text{B}\,3}$ 3 $\dfrac{\text{B} - \text{B}\,4}{\text{B} - \text{B}\,4}$ 4 $\dfrac{\text{P} - \text{Q}\,3}{\text{P} - \text{Q}\,3}$, etc.

1 $\dfrac{e\,2 - e\,4}{e\,7 - e\,5}$ 2 $\dfrac{\text{S}\,g\,1 - f\,3}{\text{S}\,b\,8 - c\,6}$ 3 $\dfrac{\text{L}f1 - c\,4}{\text{L}f8 - c\,5}$ 4 $\dfrac{d\,2 - d\,3}{d\,7 - d\,6}$, etc.

It will be observed that in the present work this form is adopted for the analysis, while the ordinary method of writing the moves opposite each other is used in the illustrative games.

It now but remains to mention an exceedingly simple method of recording positions, problems, etc. Starting at white's Q R 8 read the rank across from left to right, then the next rank, and so on down the board. White's Pieces and Pawns are denoted by capitals, Black's by small letters and the vacant squares by numbers. At the end of a rank it is convenient to draw a stroke / to save confusion by running into the next rank.

Two other useful notations, which will be used later in this book, are '?' which means 'good move' and '!' which means 'bad move'.

Chapter 6

TECHNICAL TERMS

Castles or Castling

The practice of castling is a European innovation of comparatively modern origin. In the oriental nations, the birthplace of chess, castling was unknown, and the earliest authors upon the game in Europe, Damiano (1512) and Lopez (1561) make no reference to it, but mention only the 'leap of the King', a peculiar privilege derived from the Eastern game, which permitted the King, on his being first played, provided he had not been checked, to move and even make a capture like a Knight.

Although, as a general rule, the move of the King is restricted to one square at a time, he has the privilege, under certain conditions, once in the game, of moving in conjunction with either of the Rooks two squares. This peculiar movement is called *Castling*, and is performed in the following manner: If a player wishes to castle on his King's side of the board, he simultaneously moves the King to King's Knight's square and his King's

Rook to King's Bishop's square. If he castles on the Queen's side, he simultaneously plays his King to Queen's Bishop's square, and Queen's Rook to Queen's square.

A player may not Castle: 1. If his King is in check 2. If either the King or the Castling Rook has moved 3. If the King has to move over or onto a square commanded by the enemy 4. If there is any Piece, either of his own or the adversary's, between the King and the Rook.

To show the importance of castling, to escape from an attack, and to inflict one on the adversary, refer to Figure 29. This figure illustrates the operation of Castling:

BLACK

Figure 29

WHITE

In this situation the White King is threatened with what is called 'a discovered check', that is, his opponent, by removing the Bishop would *discover* check from the Queen. Not being at the moment in check, however, and having moved neither King nor Rook, and there being no Piece between them, White may castle as indicated, incidentally giving check.

Check

The King is said to be in *check* when he is attacked by any Piece or Pawn. Though it is usual to do so, the attacking party is not obliged to announce 'check'.

Checkmate

This occurs when the attacked King cannot legally move, *i.e.* when he cannot move out of check.

Doubled Pawn

When two Pawns of the same colour are on the same file the front one is called a *doubled Pawn*.

Drawn Game

When neither party can give checkmate, the game is drawn. This may arise from several causes, as: 1st, *Perpetual check*. 2nd where there is not sufficient force to effect a mate, as a King and a Knight only, or a King and

two Knights, etc. 3rd where one party has force sufficient, but is ignorant of the proper mode of applying it,
and thus fails to checkmate his helpless adversary
within the fifty moves prescribed. 4th where both parties persist in repeating the same move from fear of each
other. 5th where both parties are left with the same
force at the end, as a Queen against a Queen, a Rook
against a Rook, and the like, when, except in particular
cases, the game should be resigned as a drawn battle.
And 6th when one of the Kings is *stalemated*.

En Prise

When a Piece or Pawn is in a situation to be taken by the
enemy, it is said to be *en prise*. To put a Piece *en prise*, is to
play it so that it may be captured.

The Exchange

When a player gains a Rook for a Bishop or a Knight, it
is termed *winning the exchange*.

False Move

Any illegal move, such as castling when the King has
been moved or is in check, moving a Rook diagonally,
or a Bishop like a Knight, is called a false or an 'impossible' move.

Fool's Mate

This is the simplest of all checkmates, being accomplished in two moves in the following manner:

WHITE	BLACK
1 P — K N 4	1 P — K 4
2 P — K B 4	2 Q — R 5, mate

It cannot possibly be given by the first player.

Forced Move

When a player has only one legal move at his or her command, it is said to be a *forced move*.

Gambit

This word is derived from an Italian phrase in wrestling, and signifies a movement by which the adversary is tripped up. In chess, this is attempted by the first player putting a Pawn *en prise* of the enemy early in the game, by which he is enabled more rapidly and effectually to develop his superior Pieces. There are several gambits, but the most important, and one which includes many others, is the King's gambit, commenced as follows:

WHITE	BLACK
1 P — K 4	1 P — K 4
2 P — K B 4	2 P × P

The Pawn offered by the first player here at his second move is called the Gambit Pawn, and when taken by the adversary the opening becomes a gambit.

■ □

The varieties of the gambits are often designated by the names of the players who invented or first brought them into vogue — as the *Muzio* gambit; the *Salvio* gambit, the *Allgaier* gambit, the *Lopez* gambit; while others obtain their names from the opening moves of the first player, as the King's Bishop's gambit, which begins thus:

WHITE	BLACK
1 P — K 4	1 P — K 4
2 P — K B 4	2 P × P
3 B — B 4	

and is so called because the King's Bishop is played out at the third move instead of the King's Knight.

There is also the Queen's gambit, of which the opening moves are:

WHITE	BLACK
1 P — Q 4	1 P — Q 4
2 P — Q B 4	2 P × P

The gambits are the most brilliant and animated of all the openings, full of hair-breadth escapes and perilous outcomes, but affording an array of daring combinations.

Giuoco Piano

A solid and instructive modification of the King's Knight's game. The opening moves are:

WHITE	BLACK
1 P — K 4	1 P — K 4
2 K N — K B 3	2 Q N — B 3
3 B — B 4	3 B — B 4

To Interpose

When the King is checked, or any valuable Piece is in danger from the attack of an enemy, you are said to *interpose* a man when you play it between the attacked and attacking Piece.

Isolated Pawn

A Pawn which stands alone, without the support and protection of other Pawns, is termed an *isolated* Pawn.

J'adoube

A French expression, signifying 'I arrange', or 'I replace', which is used by a player when he touches a man merely to adjust its position on the board, without intending to play it.

Minor Pieces

The Bishop and Knight, in contradistinction to the Queen and Rook, are called *minor Pieces*.

The Opposition

An important manoeuvre in playing the King, by which one player is enabled to occupy certain key squares, and thus compel the adverse King to abandon a favourable position.

Party

From the French *partie*. Frequently used by modern writers instead of the word 'game'.

Passed Pawn

A Pawn is said to be a *passed* one when the adversary has no Pawn to obstruct its march on the same file, or on either of the next files to the right or left.

Pion Coiffé or Marked Pawn

This is a description of odds but rarely given, and only when there is a vast disparity between the skill of the players. It consists in one party placing a *cap* or ring on one of his Pawns, and undertaking to checkmate his opponent with that particular Pawn. He is not allowed to *Queen* the Pawn, and if he loses it, or happens to checkmate his opponent with any other man, he forfeits the game. The Pawn usually *capped* is the King's Knight's, because it can be more readily and effectually surrounded by protecting Pieces.

To Queen a Pawn, or to Advance a Pawn to Queen

When a player has contrived to advance a Pawn to the eighth or last square of the file, it assumes the rank and power of a Queen, or any other Piece he chooses, and he is then said to have *Queened* his Pawn.

Scholar's Mate

A checkmate occasionally given at the opening of a game by a practised player to one but little tutored in the science. The following are the moves:

WHITE	BLACK
1 P — K 4	1 P — K 4
2 B — B 4	2 B — B 4
3 Q — R 5	3 P — Q 3
4 Q × P, mate	

Smothered Mate

A checkmate which is sometimes given by the Knight, when the adverse King is hemmed in, or *smothered*, by his own forces. (See Figure 33).

Stalemate

When one party has his King so circumstanced that not being at the moment in check, he cannot play him without going into check, and at the same time has no other Piece or Pawn to move instead, he is said to be *stalemated,* and the game is considered drawn. (See Figure 34).

Taking a Pawn En Passant, or In Passing

It has been shown before, in speaking of the action of the Pawn, that he is limited in his march to one square forward at a time, when not capturing, and one square forward diagonally, either to the right or left, when he takes an adversary, but that he has the privilege, on being first played in the game, to advance two squares, unless in so doing he passes a square which is attacked by a hostile Pawn; in which case the opponent may, at his option, permit him to make the two steps forward, and there remain, or may capture him in his passage in the same way as if he had moved but one step. (See Figure 26.)

Checkmate

BLACK

Figure 30

WHITE

Above is an example of mate. White plays Q × P ch. Black can now only save his King in two ways, either by taking White's Q with his P, or by interposing his B. If Black plays P × Q, White replies with B —N 6 mate — since Black cannot move his King out of check, nor interpose a Piece, nor take White's Bishop. If instead of taking the Q, Black had interposed his B by playing it to K 2, White would simply take the B with his Q, giving mate again. Black cannot take White's Q, for it is protected by a Bishop.

Discovered Check and Checkmate

BLACK

Figure 31

WHITE

The above diagram illustrates both *discovered check,* and also *checkmate.* White has the move, and it will be seen that his own Rook prevents his Bishop from attacking the Black King. He therefore plays R — N 6 giving *discovered check*. Black cannot move his King out of check, he must therefore *interpose* his Queen on N 2, between his own King and the White Bishop. White now plays R × R *mate* — since Black cannot take the Rook nor interpose any piece between it and his King.

Perpetual Check

BLACK

Figure 32

WHITE

This position is a modification of the preceding one, to illustrate *perpetual check*. White has the move, and having less force than Black is satisfied to get a drawn game. He therefore plays Q — B 6 check. Black cannot move his King out of check, so therefore he must interpose his Queen again on N 2. White now plays Q — K8 check, and Black, still not being able to move his King out of check, must bring back his Queen to N 1, and White repeats the previous move, thus giving perpetual check and gaining a draw.

Smothered Mate

BLACK

Figure 33

WHITE

This is a familiar example of *smothered mate,* which you will find can be effected by no other Piece than the Knight. White's first move is, Queen to her 5th square, checking. Black is obliged to retreat his King to the Rook's square, because, were he to play him to his Bishop's square, the Queen would checkmate at once. Upon the King retiring, White gives check with his Knight at K B 7; this brings the King back again to Knight's square, and affords to White an opportunity of giving *double check,* which he does by moving the Knight to K R 6, checking with both Queen and Knight; as before, the King must go to Rook's square; and now follows a beautiful move — White plays his Queen down to *K N 8* (next square to the Black King), giving check; the King cannot take on account of the Knight;

he is compelled, therefore, to capture with his Rook, and the Knight then gives the *smothered mate* at K B 7.

Stalemate

BLACK

Figure 34

WHITE

White has the move. He cannot move his Queen from in front of his King, for then the latter would be in check. He has nothing better to do than to take Black's Rook, but then the latter is stalemated, since his King is not in check. He cannot move it without going into check, and he has no other move.

Chapter 7

RELATIVE VALUE OF THE CHESS PIECES

An attempt to establish a scale of powers whereby the relative values of the men could be estimated with mathematical exactitude, although it has frequently engaged the attention of scientific minds, appears to be an unattainable object. So ever varying, so much dependant on the mutations of *position* which every move occasions, and on the augmented power which it acquires when combined with other forces, is the proportionate worth of this with that particular man, that it would seem to be beyond the reach of computation to devise a formula by which it can be reckoned with precision. But still an approximation to correctness has been made, and the result arrived at gives the following as the ultimate respective values:

Pawn	= 1.00
Knight	= 3.05
Bishop	= 3.50
Rook	= 5.48
Queen	= 9.94

■ ☐

The King, from the nature of the game, which does not allow his being exchanged or captured, is invaluable, and he is not, therefore, included in the calculations.

The Pawn, it is seen, is the least valuable of all the men, the Knight being worth at least three Pawns.

The Bishops and Knights are practically considered of equal value, although there is a difference in the estimate here given.

A Rook is of the value of five Pawns and a fraction, and may be exchanged for a minor Piece and two Pawns. Two Rooks may be exchanged for three minor Pieces.

The Queen is usually reckoned equal, in average situations, to two Rooks and a Pawn, but towards the end of a game she is hardly so valuable as two Rooks.

These comparative values may be of service to the student in general cases of exchanging men, but he will find in practice the relative worth of his soldiers is modified by so many circumstances of time, opportunity, and position, that nothing but experience can ever teach accurately in every case 'which to give up and which to keep'.

Chapter 8

LAWS OF THE GAME

T he following Laws, with some variations, have been in general use for the last hundred years. They have been embodied in the British Chess Code, and are now universally adopted by all the chess clubs of Great Britain.

1 The chess-board must be so placed that each player has a white square at his right-hand corner of the board. If the board has been improperly placed, either player may require the game to be annulled, provided the game has not been finished, and that *four* moves on each side have not been played, but not afterwards.

2 If a Piece or Pawn be misplaced at the beginning of the game, either player may require the game to be annulled, if it is not finished, and before the second player has played his fourth move, but not afterwards.

3 Should a player, at the commencement of the game, omit to place all his men on the board, either

player may require the game to be annulled, if it is not finished, and before the second player has played his fourth move, but not afterwards.

4   If a player, undertaking to give the odds of a Piece or Pawn, neglects to remove it from the board, his adversary, after four moves have been played on each side, has the choice of proceeding with or recommencing the game.

5   When no odds are given, the players must take the first move of each game alternately, drawing lots to determine who shall begin the first game. Unless otherwise arranged, the first player in each game shall take White.

6   The player who gives the odds has the right of moving first in each game, unless otherwise agreed. Where a Pawn, Knight, Bishop or Rook is conceded, unless otherwise agreed it shall be the King's Bishop's Pawn, the Queen's Knight, the Queen's Bishop, or the Queen's Rook.

7   A Piece or Pawn touched must be played, unless immediately before touching it the player announces his intention of adjusting it; *but if a Piece or Pawn be displaced by accident, it may be restored to its place without penalty.*

8   While a player holds the Piece or Pawn he has touched, he play it to any other than the square he took it from; but, having quitted it, he cannot recall the move.

9   Should a player touch one of his adversary's Pieces or Pawns, other than for adjusting it, his adversary may compel him to take it; but if it cannot be legally taken, he may oblige him to move the King; if his King, however, cannot be legally moved, his opponent may indicate a man which he must move.

10   If a player takes one of his adversary's men with one of his own that cannot legally take it, his antagonist may require him to replace the man, and then (*a*) take it with a legal move if he can; (*b*)if he cannot, then to move his King; (*c*) if he cannot move his King, his opponent can indicate a Piece to be moved.

11   Should a player take one of his own men with another, his adversary has the option of obliging him to move either.

12   If a player makes an illegal move, his opponent may require him to (*a*) move that man legally; (*b*) or if he cannot, move his King; (*c*) if he cannot move his King, his opponent can indicate a Piece to be moved.

13   Should a player move out of his turn, his adversary may require him to replace the man and then when his turn to play comes, (*a*) move it; or (*b*) if he cannot, move his King; or (*c*) if he cannot move his King, his opponent can indicate a man to be moved.

14   When a Pawn is first moved in a game, it may be played one or two squares; but in the latter case the opponent has the privilege of taking it *en passant* with any Pawn which could have taken it had it been played one square only. A Pawn cannot be taken *en passant* by a Piece. See page 76.

15 A player cannot castle in the following cases:
1. If the King or Rook have been moved.
2. If the King be in check.
3. If there be any Piece between the King and Rook.
4. If the King passes over any square attacked by one of the adversary's Pieces or Pawns. See page 68.

16 If a player touches a Piece or Pawn that cannot be moved without leaving the King in check, he must replace the Piece or Pawn and move his King; but if the King cannot be moved, he may be required to move a man selected by his opponent.

17 Every Pawn which has reached the eighth or last square on the chess-board, must be immediately exchanged for a Queen or any other Piece (of the same colour) the player may think fit, even though all the Pieces remain on the board. It follows, therefore, that he may have two or more Queens, three or more Rooks, Bishops, or Knights.

18 A player may claim a game as drawn if he can prove that the last fifty moves on each side have been made without a Pawn being moved or a Piece taken.

19 If a player agrees to checkmate with a particular Piece or Pawn, or on a particular square, or engage to force his adversary to stalemate or checkmate him, he is not restricted to any number of moves.

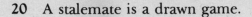
20   A stalemate is a drawn game.

21   If a player makes an illegal move, the adversary must take notice of such irregularity before he touches a Piece or Pawn, or he will not be allowed to inflict any penalty.

Chapter 9

GENERAL RULES AND OBSERVATIONS

Concerning the King

I t is generally advisable to castle the King early in the game, and to do so on the King's side, because he is less subject to an attack, and better able to repel one on that side than the other — nevertheless, it frequently happens, that a player by castling on the Queen's side, is enabled to make a formidable assault on the adverse King, by throwing forward his King's flank Pawns. When the Queens are exchanged off early in the game, it is often well to move the King to K B 2, and in that way bring the Rooks into play, instead of castling, because there is then less danger to the King, and he may become a valuable auxiliary during the remainder of the fight. In castling, move the King before you touch the Rook.

■ □

Be fearful, when castled on the King's side, of permitting an adverse Knight to gain safe possession of your K B 4 square, and remember that it is seldom prudent in an inexperienced player to advance the Pawns on the side on which his King has castled.

Be cautious of playing your Queen in front of your King. Never subject yourself to a discovered check. It is better when check is given to your King to interpose a man that attacks the checking Piece than with one which does not. Beware of giving useless checks to your adversary's King, but when, by checking, you can oblige him to move, and thus deprive him of the right to castle, it is generally good play to do so. It is sometimes useful to give a series of checks, and even sacrifice a Piece, to force the King into the middle of the board, where he may be subjected to the attacks of your other men.

Do not in all cases take an enemy's Pawn which stands before your King — it may serve sometimes as a protection to him; and bear in mind that towards the termination of a game, especially when the superior Pieces have been taken off the board, the King should be made to compensate for his previous inactivity, by being busily engaged. The fate of the game is then dependent for the most part on the skill displayed in the management of the King.

Concerning the Queen

The Queen is so powerful and important a Piece at chess that she should rarely be employed to defend or attack any point if you can do it as well with a subordinate.

It is not good to play the Queen out into the game at the beginning, because she can be attacked by inferior Pieces, and is compelled to retire with the loss of many moves.

Be careful, too, when about to capture a distant Pawn or Piece, that you do not remove your Queen too far from the immediate point of action. A clever player will often permit you to win a Pawn with the Queen, that he may prevent her returning in time to rescue your King from his attack. The power of the Queen is wonderfully greater when she is aided and protected by other Pieces than when she goes forth unsupported; it is generally injudicious, therefore, to make an attack with her unless in combination with some other of your forces.

Concerning the Rook

The Rook is a most important officer, yet few players even among the best avail themselves sufficiently of his power. He has seldom much scope for action in the early part of the engagement, but when the field is thinned no time should be lost in bringing him into action. You should then endeavour to *double* your Rooks, that is, to place them one before the other on the same file: in this situation, mutually sustaining one another, their power on a clear board is equal to the Queen's — sometimes superior.

It is usually good play to get command of an open file, that is to say, a file which is occupied by no other man, by stationing a Rook at one end of it. When you have thus gained possession of the file, should your opponent try to dispossess you of it, by playing one of his Rooks on to the same file, it is frequently better to defend with your other Rook than to take his or remove your own. You will often embarrass your adversary, too, if you can manage to post a Rook on his second rank, say at your K 7 or Q 7. In this position he generally makes an attack on the Pawns unmoved, and compels the enemy to lose time defending them, while you can bring more forces into action.

One of the strongest reasons for playing out your Pieces early in the battle, is, that while at home they are not only themselves inactive, but they utterly retard the movements of your Rooks. In an unskilfully developed game it is a common occurrence to see the victory won before the defeated player's Rooks have been moved.

Concerning the Bishop

When the game is opened by each party with P — K 4, the King's Bishop is somewhat superior to the Queen's because it can be sooner brought into play, and may be made to bear immediately on the adversary's weak point, the K B P. It is desirable therefore generally to exchange your Q B or Q N for the adversary's K B. The K B should rarely or never be played to the Q 3 before the Queen's Pawn is moved. His best position, as we have remarked above, is Q B 4, where he attacks the opponent's K B P. If your antagonist then challenges an exchange of Bishops by moving B — K 3, it is not always prudent to accept it, because although you may double the Pawns on his King's file, you at the same time afford him an open range for his King's Rook, when he has castled. The best play in such a case is, therefore, to retreat your B to N 3.

Be careful, as a general rule, in an open game, not to move P — Q 3 *before* you bring out the K B, as by so doing he can only be played to K 2, and there his position is defensive rather than attacking.

If strong in Pawns towards the conclusion of the game, endeavour to get rid of the enemy's Bishops, because they can impede the march of your Pawns more readily than either the Rooks or Knights.

When the other men are exchanged off, and you remain with a Bishop and two or three Pawns, it is often proper to keep your Pawns on squares of a different colour to those on which your Bishop travels, as he can then prevent the opposing King from approaching them. If, however, you have the worst of the game, it is generally better then to keep them on the same colour as the Bishop, that he may defend them.

Supposing you have Pawns only at the end of a game, and the adversary has a Bishop, it is generally advisable to move the Pawns to squares of a different colour to the Bishop.

Do not indiscriminately exchange your Bishops for Knights, or *vice versa*. Two Bishops at the finish of a game are stronger than two Knights, and one Knight generally more useful than a single Bishop.

Concerning the Knight

The Knight is at once the most striking and most beautiful of all the Pieces. The singularity of its moves, by

■ □

which it is enabled to overleap the other men and wind its way into the adverse ranks, and if attacked leap back again within the boundary of its own, has rendered it the favourite Piece of leading players in every country.

The assault of the Knight is more subtle and dangerous than that of any other Piece, because he attacks without putting himself *en prise,* and his attack can never be resisted by the interposition of another man.

At the commencement of a game, the best place for the King's Knight is at K B 3; it there attacks your adversary's King's Pawn, if it has been played to K 4, and offers no impediment to the playing out of your King's Bishop, and prevents the adversary from placing his Queen on K R 5, where she would often be a source of restraint and danger to your King. Many persons prefer playing the N to K 2 at the second move, from the mistaken notion that the K B P should be moved before the Knight is played to B 3; this is an error, and generally leads to a bad game.

When you have brought out your Q N to B 3, it is frequently advisable, at a proper opportunity, to get him round via K 2 to K N 3, where he exercises a very important influence, by threatening N — B 5.

Other things being equal, a Knight with three or four Pawns, at the end of a game, has an advantage over a Bishop with an equal number of Pawns, because he can leap from white to black, and thus attack the Pawns on either coloured squares, whereas the Bishop can attack them only when they move on squares of the colour of his diagonals. In similar circumstances, however, he is not so useful in defending as a Bishop or a Rook, since if forced to remove he ceases to defend, while the Rook or Bishop may retreat and still protect.

Concerning the Pawns

Struck by the scope and power of the higher Pieces, young players commonly overlook the Pawns, or deem them scarcely worthy of regard, and are amazed to learn that the combinations of these simple elements are among the most refined and arduous studies of the game. Yet such is the fact, and without a thorough comprehension of their quiet but remarkable predominance in almost every circumstance of the game, it is impossible for anyone to attain a high degree of excellence.

It is generally advantageous for your Pawns to occupy the middle of the board, because when there they greatly retard the movements of the opposing forces. The K P and Q P at K 4 and Q 4 respectively, are well posted, but it is not easy to maintain them in that position, and if you are driven to advance one of them, the power of both is much diminished. It is well, therefore, not to be too eager to establish two Pawns abreast in the centre until you are fully able to sustain them there.

When you have two Pawns abreast, as at K 4 and Q 4, should the adversary attack one of them with a Pawn, it is occasionally better to advance the Pawn that is attacked than to take the Pawn.

The Pawns, however, should seldom be far advanced, unless they can be properly sustained by the Pieces. Pawns at their fourth squares are therefore generally more powerful than at their sixth.

The K B P, having no support but that of the King, is usually the point to which the first attack is directed, and more than ordinary care should be taken to preserve it. It is rarely good play to move it to B 3 early in the game.

As a general rule it is not advisable to move the Knight's Pawns early in the game. P — K N 3 will often allow your adversary to play his Q B — R 6, a dangerous move when you have castled on the King's side.

After castling, it is proper not to move the Knight's Pawn that is before your King, until you are obliged.

In a diagonal line of Pawns you should endeavour to preserve the Pawn at the head of them. Pawns, when united, have great strength; but when separated, their power is much lessened.

A passed Pawn is greatly strengthened when supported by another Pawn.

A doubled Pawn is not always a disadvantage, especially if united with other Pawns. The worst kind of doubled Pawn is one on a Rook's file; while the most advantageous is the K B P doubled on the King's file, it strengthens your middle Pawns and opens a file for your K R.

The Pawn being less important than a Piece, it is usually better to defend with it than with a Piece. For the same reason it is likewise better to protect a Pawn with a Pawn than with a Piece. No Piece can interpose between the attack of a Pawn, it can therefore frequently check the King with great advantage.

Be cautious generally of advancing the Pawns far on either side, till you see on which your opponent castles; and remember, when approaching the end of a game, where you have Pawns, or even a Pawn, against a minor Piece, that *you may win,* but that your opponent, except in very rare cases, cannot, and that two Pawns in any situation can protect themselves against the adverse King.

Chapter 10

MAXIMS AND ADVICE FOR BEGINNERS

T here is nothing that will improve you so much as playing with good players; never refuse, therefore, when anyone offers you odds, to accept it; you cannot expect a good player to feel much interested in playing with you upon even terms, and as you are sure to derive both amusement and instruction from him, it is but fair that he should name the conditions. It will soon happen that you yourself will be able to give odds to many amateurs whom you meet; when this is the case, avoid, if possible, playing them even, or you are likely to acquire an indolent, neglectful habit of play, which it will be very difficult to throw off. Be always careful, before beginning a game, that the men on both sides are properly arranged.

Never permit your hand to hover over the board, or indeed to approach it, until you have completely made

■ □

up your mind what Piece to move; a contrary habit begets a feeling of indecision that is fatal to success. Play invariably according to the laws of the game, neither taking back a move yourself, nor allowing your opponent to recall one. Do not exhibit impatience when your adversary is long in making his move. His slowness is a tacit compliment to your skill, and enables you to play with proportionate quickness, because while he is meditating on his next step you can take advantage of the time to consider what shall be your rejoinder; besides, it is absolutely necessary for every one desirous of excelling at chess to play slowly.

Learn to play indifferently either with the white or black men. Do not play too many games at a sitting — and never suffer the loss of a game to occasion you much disquietude. The loss of one well-fought game with a fine player will do more towards your improvements than the gain of ten light skirmishes with weaker players than yourself. Endeavour to play all your Pieces equally well. Many young players have a predilection for a particular Piece, as the Knight or Queen, and lose both time and position in trying to prevent exchanges of their favourite. In opening your game, endeavour to bring the Pieces into action speedily, but avoid all premature attacks. Take care not to play a Piece to a square where it impedes the action of another, and beware of venturing an unsupported Piece in the adversary's game.

If subjected to a violent attack, you may often disconcert your opponent by compelling the exchange of two or three Pieces. When, however, you are about to exchange, you must calculate not only their ordinary value, but their peculiar worth in the situation in question; for example, a Rook is generally more valuable than a Knight or a Bishop; but it may happen, that by exchanging a Rook for one of the latter you may greatly improve your game.

It is generally good play to exchange the Pieces off when you are superior in power, so that when you have the odds of a Piece given to you by a strong player, you should endeavour to exchange as often as you can consistently with safety.

When an exchange of two or more Pieces appears inevitable, look closely to see whether it is better for you to take first or to compel your opponent to do so. When one of the enemy is completely in your power, do not be too eager to make the capture — there may perhaps be a move of importance which you can make before you take him. Beware also of snatching hastily a proffered man, it may be only given as a bait to catch a more important advantage from you.

If at the end of a game you remain with Pawns against a Knight and find it difficult to evade his repeated checks, recollect that by placing your King on the same diagonal as the Knight, but with one intervening square between them, that you cannot again be checked under three moves.

When you have lost a game which has cost you great attention, it is a good practice to play it over afterwards in private, and endeavour to discover where the error occurred through which your opponent gained his first advantage. This custom will improve both your memory and your play.

Appearances notwithstanding, chess is an exciting

game. This is perhaps the most surprising feature that the beginner, who had thought it so dull, will notice. It will cause many of his blunders. First-class players lose 'won' games every day by reason of it. So that it is extremely important for the student to acquire as much self-command as he possibly can from the very commencement of his chess career. So important is this that Steinitz, for twenty-eight years chess champion of the world, laid it down as a rule for himself, that whenever he saw a good move he did not take it — until he had looked all over the board for a better. Even Steinitz felt the necessity for checking himself from making hasty moves. Good moves are not at all obvious; in fact, the reverse is a pretty general rule. Hence they will not be easily seen, and least of all by those in a hurry. Beginners, therefore, take time, *even when you see a mate on the move.* Mates are elusive, and a would-be mating move is often the turning point in the novice's game. Caution should be borne in mind throughout the entire game, but particularly at the climax when coolness may be worth a piece to the player who possesses it.

Join a club. Practically no progress will be made by playing with friends at home, and often a very bad style is acquired by too frequently meeting the same opponent.

Some players pore over the board all the time, whether it is their turn to play or not. Others never look at the position till it is their turn to move. A judicious compromise of these extremes is probably best. While waiting for your opponent during a long game it is often advantageous to divert your mind completely for a few minutes by strolling round the room or otherwise, and then come back to the board with a fresh aspect of the position. It is then often seen to contain possibilities that you did not see before.

Always play against the board; that is, give your opponent credit for playing the best move every time, and try and meet it accordingly. Even when you know your opponent to be a weak player do not take liberties with him which his calibre might justify, but — just play, not him, but the board. His little fusilades will be futile enough, and against correct play he will soon succumb. This is not easy to do; especially where there is great disparity between the players. The stronger is often inclined to take risks in order to win quickly, trusting to the inability of his opponent to take advantage of them. This is unwise, for it induces the habit of loose play, and the day will come when you will take the risks — and the other fellow the game. When your opponent moves, before you put your own ideas into effect, try and see the object of his move. This will be most difficult to do against very strong and very weak players. The very strong will be too deep — the very weak purposeless. For the object of the former you may, and for the latter you certainly will, look in vain. When you see his idea, fortify yourself against it before proceeding with your attack, unless you are absolutely sure you can mate him before he can you, when you may disregard his move — except of course if it is a check. Do not be discouraged by players who, when defeated, exclaim, 'If I had been just a move sooner I would have had you'. They are found in every club.

In playing weak players do not study their tactics, except as things to be avoided. If your opponent reconnoitres the board exhaustively with a solitary Knight, he is giving you every opportunity to gain time — and possibly the Knight also.

To play chess well demands patience and restraint. The man who easily loses heart or head will never make a strong player. It is beautiful to watch a resourceful player who, after early reverses, drags the remnants of a shattered attack together, welds a number of disunited pieces and pawns by combination into a position that ultimately allows him to enter the end game on equal terms with his opponent. Such a player will go far, and his reverses will become beautifully less.

Strength at chess may be variously acquired. Natural insight and continuous hard practice produce the greatest players. A few of these may rightly be regarded as geniuses, but it would be a mistake to say that every man who achieved master rank was. A natural gift for the game is easily detected. It will manifest itself among beginners by original, unexpected moves, even though they may be unsound. But the surest sign that a player has natural chess capacity is to note that, after being shown once or twice *why* a bad move in the openings is bad, how carefully he eschews that move in future. The mere wood shifter will make the same blunder a thousand times; not indeed because he does not *know* that it is wrong — for he has often been told so — but simply because he cannot see *why* it is so. Thus, after playing:

1 P — K 4	P — K 4
2 B — B 4	B — B 4
3 Q — R 5	

the gifted beginner will only require to be shown a couple of times why **3. Q — R 5** is useless, but your stubborn fellow will persist in his futile attempts to take your King unawares.

If in the opening you find that your opponent has moved seven men in seven moves, and you have only moved two, be sure you will soon find out an alarming difference in your positions. You have been doing much wood shifting with very little progress.

An excellent way for gaining all round insight into position and at the same time learning the openings is the habit of playing over master games. It is hardly possible to overrate the value of this pleasant though little-practised pastime. It is far better, and often more enjoyable, than playing with beginners, and, done systematically, improves one's play immensely. The handiest way is perhaps to play with a pocket board, but of course any board will do. Two methods may be followed. First, put yourself on the side of the winning party and study the development of *his* game, giving less attention to the other side, for practice has shown that it is not advisable to try and keep in touch with both sides at the same time. Cover the score of the side you are playing, say White, and after every move of Black try and discover what White's reply will be before looking at the score. At first you will not divine many of his moves, but later on, you will be gratified to see how often you would have played the same move in such and such a position. The deep moves alone will elude you, but even these will occasionally be discovered.

The second plan is to take one player to yourself as before, but do not look whether he has won or lost the game. Cover the score. Then, during the progress of the play try and see how he is faring — you not knowing the result. Practice will enable you in time to recognize a gradual advantage (or the reverse) which he may have accumulated. It is the ability to recognize such changes in position that makes the good player.

Games of the old masters are unsurpassed for brilliancy of combination and middle game play generally. In playing over games, especially those of modern experts, the student will incidentally acquire a sound knowledge of the openings. An interesting feature in playing recorded games is to note the characteristics of various exponents. As in literature so in chess, every master has his style. Some play the open, some play the close game. Some are content to attempt nothing, keeping the draw well in sight, and hoping for their opponent to make a slight mistake. The enterprising, however, will set out on a plan of attack, and court intricacies. They will even sacrifice material to produce a position after their fancy. These variations are possible, because chess puts no limit on a person's fancy, and individual — even national — traits, find expression in the game as in music. Thus the modern school, led by the Germans, is sound, deep and theoretically correct. The Italian school, on the other hand, is more brilliant and showy, though not so accurate and lasting. The highest expression of chess skill is a judicious combination of the two.

Another good plan for strengthening play, and more exciting than it sounds, is correspondence chess. This is specially to be commended to players living in out-of-the-way parts of the country, where it is not easy to get a game over the board. It generates the habit of deliberate play, particularly with those who rightly *think out* some of the minor variations, rather than playing them all over the board, before despatching a move.

If the student will bear some of these hints in mind he will be surprised to find that the study of chess, commonly regarded as both dull and slow, can be made both interesting and rapid. His progress need meet with no checks, for chess itself is inexhaustible. The only limit it knows are those of the human mind. So that at chess a person may demonstrate his superiority against all the world more conclusively, perhaps, than at any other game.

Comparing small things with great ones, never forget that in chess, as in modern warfare, one of the most important stratagems is the art of gaining *time* upon the enemy. In this respect, as indeed in many others, the broad principles which are laid down by the highest military authorities as the basis of operations in a campaign are applicable to the management of your forces on the chess field. From the *Traité de Grand Tactique* of General Jomini, we gather that the art of war, as exemplified by Buonaparte, consisted in the proper application of three combinations — first, the art of disposing the lines of operation in the most advantageous manner; secondly, in a skilful concentration of the forces with the greatest possible rapidity upon the most important point of the enemy's line of operations; and thirdly, that of combining the simultaneous employment of this accumulated force upon the position against which it is directed. No player of great skill can fail to see that we have here the key to the basis of offensive movements in the battle of chess. Nor, to carry on the parallel, are the principles which direct defensive operations on the grander field in any degree less capable of application. 'It is an acknowledged principle,' says another able writer on the subject, 'that the base of a plan of attack should form the best possible line of defence; and this fundamental rule cannot be violated with impunity, since nothing is more embarrassing than a sudden transition from offensive to defensive operations, when false measures or an unfortunate turn of affairs may have overset the plans of an assault.'

With every allowance for the amazing disparity in the importance of the individuals and the magnitude of the objects at stake, there is an analogy observable, too, in the abilities requisite for the command of armies and the perfectly first-rate manoeuvring of the mimic warriors of the chess-board. The commander of an army must possess not less a profound acquaintance with the general principles which regulate the conduct of a long and tedious campaign, than with those that are called into requisition in actual conflict. He must be able equally to arrange the plan of preliminary operations —to act at once and with decision in cases of the most pressing emergency, and on the occurrence of the most unforeseen events — to judge of the importance of a position and of the strength of an entrenchment — to discover from the slightest indications the designs of the enemy, while his own are impenetrable — and at the same time to preside with unshaken self-possession over the tumult of the battle-field, and the raging fury of an assault. The qualifications of a really finished chess-player, however less in degree, are somewhat similar in kind. To a perfect mastery of the difficult art of selecting and occupying, with the utmost rapidity, a 'good position', he must add a thorough knowledge of all the complicated varieties and stratagems and snares which he is called upon alternately to invent and to defeat. He must, in short, to some extent, display the same energies on the smaller scale which are so indispensable on the grander one.

Marshal Saxe, a great general (and an enthusiastic lover of chess, by the way), in his summary of the attributes required in a commander-in-chief, gives him genius, and courage, and health. The first of these qualities is unquestionably called for in the highest order of chess skill; and if by courage is implied, not so much mere physical bravery as entire self-possession, promptitude of decision, and undaunted perseverance; and by health is meant the preservation of a sound mind, to which a sound body is so important an adjunct, then indeed both courage and health will be found to exercise a powerful influence upon the success of the chess-player, as well as upon the fortunes of a Marlborough or a Wellington.

These comparisons might be extended to more minute particulars, but the general analogy may suffice to show you that great mental activity is called for, and much attention and perseverance are necessary for the attainment of the highest excellence, in the strategy of chess-playing.

Chapter 11

PRELIMINARY GAME

P reparatory to the investigation of the different openings examined in the following chapters, it may not be uninstructive to give a short game which will exhibit the application of some technical phrases used in chess, and at the same time show a few of the most prominent errors into which an inexperienced player is likely to fall.

In this game, as in all the analyses which follow, the reader will be supposed to play the White Pieces and to have the first move, although, as it has been before remarked, it is advisable for you to accustom yourself to play with either Black or White.

WHITE	BLACK
1 P — K 4	P — K 4

When the men are first arranged in battle order, it is seen that the only Pieces which have the power of moving are the Knights, and that to liberate the others it is necessary to move a Pawn. Now, as the K P, on being moved, gives freedom both to the Q and the K B, it is more frequently played at the beginning of the game than any other. You will remember, in speaking of the Pawns it was shown that on certain conditions they have the privilege of going either one or two moves when they are first played.

2	B — B 4	B — B 4

Thus far the game illustrates the *King's Bishop's* opening. Each party plays his K B thus, because it attacks the most vulnerable point of the adverse position, viz. the K B P.

3	P — Q B 3	N — Q B 3

In playing this Pawn your object is afterwards to play P — Q 4, and thus establish your Pawns in the centre; but Black foresees the intention and seeks to prevent its execution by bringing another Piece to bear upon the square.

4	P — Q 4	P × P
5	P × P	B × P

Here you have played without due consideration. Black's third move of N — Q B 3 was a bad one, and afforded you an opportunity of gaining a striking advantage, but omitting this, you have enabled him to gain a valuable Pawn for nothing. Observe, now, your reply to his third move was good enough (4 P — Q 4), but when he took your Pawn with his, instead of taking again, you ought to have played B × P ch.; the game would then most probably have gone on thus:

5	B × P ch.	K × B
6	Q — R 5 ch.	K — B 1
7	Q × B ch.	

In this variation, you see Black has lost his K B P, and what is worse, *has lost his privilege of castling,* by being forced to move his King; and although for a moment he had gained a Bishop for a Pawn, it was quite clear that he must lose a Bishop in return by the check of the adverse Queen. It is true that he need not have taken the Bishop, but still his King must have moved, and White could then have played B × N, having the better position.

But now to proceed with the actual game:

6 N — K B 3   Q — B 3

Bringing out the Knight is good play; you not only threaten to win his Bishop, but you afford yourself an opportunity of castling whenever it may be needful. Black would have played better in retiring the Bishop to N 3 than in supporting it with the Queen.

7 N × B   Q × N

Both parties played well in their last moves. Your rightly took off the Bishop, because supported by the Queen he menaced your Q N P, and Black properly retook with his Queen instead of with the Knight, because having a Pawn ahead, it was in his interest to exchange off the Queens.

8 N — Q 2   N — B 3

You played correctly here in not exchanging Queens, and also in protecting your Bishop and your King's Pawn, both of which were attacked by the adverse Queen; but all this might have been done without impeding the movements of any of your Pieces, by simply playing Q — K 2; as it is, the Knight entirely shuts

your Queen's Bishop from the field. Black properly
brings another Piece to the attack of your King's
Pawn:

9   P — B 3   N — K 4

In protecting the Pawn with your K B P you are guilty of
a very common error among young players; as you
improve, you will find that it is rarely good to play
P— K B 3. In the present instance, for example, you
have deprived yourself of the power of castling, at least
for some time, since Black's Queen now commands the
very square to which your King, in castling on his own
side, has to move. Black's last move is much more sensible. He again attacks your Bishop, and by the same
move brings his Q's Knight into cooperation with the
King's, on the weak point of your position:

10   P — Q N 3   Q × R

This is a serious blunder indeed. In your anxiety to save
the threatened Bishop, which you feared to withdraw to
N 3, on account of Black playing N — Q 6 ch., you have
actually left your Rook *en prise!* Black takes it, of course,
and having gained such an important advantage, ought
to win easily.

11   0 — 0   N × B
12   N × N   0 — 0
13   Q — Q 2   P — B 4

Your last move is very subtle; finding the mistake that
Black had committed in not retreating his Queen directly after winning the Rook, you determine, if possible,
to prevent her escape by gaining command of all the
squares she can move to. Seeing the danger, Black

throws forward this Pawn to enable him, if possible, to bring the Queen off, by playing Q — Q 5 ch.

| 14 | B — N 2 | Q × P |

This move of the Bishop is well-timed: it does not, to be sure, prevent the Queen from escaping for a move or two, but it gives you an attack, and very great command of the field.

| 15 | Q — N 5 | N — K 1 |

Very well played on both sides. By playing Q — N 5 you threatened to win his Knight by at once taking it with your Bishop, which he could not retake without opening check on his King. Instead of so moving, you might have played N — R 5, in which case, by afterwards moving R — R 1, it would have been impossible for his Queen to get away.

| 16 | Q — K 3 | P — K R 3 |

You prudently retreated your Queen to guard her Knight's Pawn, which it was important to save, on account of its protection to the Knight. Black played P — K R 3 to prevent your Queen returning to the same post of attack.

| 17 | P — R 3 | K — R 1 |

Here are two instances of what is called 'lost time' at chess, neither move serving in the slightest degree to advance the game of the player. That you should have overlooked the opportunity of gaining the adverse Queen (by R — R 1) was to be expected. Similar advantages present themselves in every game between young players, and are unobserved.

| 18 | P — B 4 | P — Q N 3 |

Again you have failed to see a most important move; you might have taken the R P with your Queen, giving check safely, because Black could not take your Queen, as his P is 'pinned' by your B. All this time, too, your opponent omits to see the jeopardy his Queen is in, and that as far as practical assistance to his other pieces is concerned, she might as well be off the board.

| 19 | P — K N 4 | P — Q N 4 |

Your last move is far from good. By thus attacking your Knight, Black threatens to win a Piece, because upon playing away the Knight you must leave the Bishop unprotected.

| 20 | P — N 5 | P × N |

Although your Knight was thus attacked, it might have been saved very easily. In the first place, by Q × P, threatening to take his Rook, on his removing which, or interposing the Q P, you could have taken the Pawn which attacked your Knight; or, in the second place, by moving your Queen to B 2. In the latter case, if Black ventured to take the Knight, you would have won his Queen by B × P ch. Black would have been obliged to parry the check, either by taking the Bishop or moving his King, and you would then have taken his Queen. This position is very instructive, and merits attentive examination.

| 21 | B — B 3 | P × Q N P |
| 22 | P — R 4 | P — N 7 |

In such a position, the advance of your King's flank Pawns is a process too dilatory to be very effective.

23	P — B 5	P — N 8 (Q)

Now the fault of your tortoise-like movements with the Pawns becomes fatally evident. Black has been enabled to make a second Queen, and has an overwhelming force at his command.

24	R × Q	Q × R ch.

You had no better move than to take the newly-elected Queen, for two Queens must have proved irresistible.

25	K — N 2	N — Q 3
26	P — N 6	P × P
27	P × P	B — N 2

Here you have given another remarkable instance of lost opportunity. At your last move you might have redeemed all former disasters by checkmating your opponent in two moves. Endeavour to find out how this was to be accomplished.

28	P — R 5	N × P
29	B — K 5	N — N 4 ch.

Up to Black's last move you had still the opportunity of winning the game before mentioned.

30	K — N 3	R — B 6 ch.
31	K — R 4	Q — B 4

At this point you were utterly at the mercy of your antagonist, but fortunately he wanted the skill to avail himself properly of his vast superiority in force and position, or he might have won the game in half a dozen different ways.

32	Q × R	Q × Q
33	B × P ch.	K × B

This was your last chance, and its success should serve to convince you that in the most apparently hopeless situations of the game there is often a latent resource, if we will only have the patience to search it out. By taking the Bishop, Black has left your King, which is not in check, no move without going into check, and as you have neither Piece nor Pawn besides to play, you are *stalemated,* and the game is drawn.

Four Chess Problems for Learners

PROBLEM No. 1

BLACK

Figure 35

White to play and mate in two moves

PROBLEM No. 2

BLACK

Figure 36

White to play and mate in three moves

PROBLEM No. 3

BLACK

Figure 37

White to play and mate in two moves

PROBLEM No. 4

BLACK

Figure 38

White to play and mate in two moves

Harder Chess Problems

Chess problems form a branch of the game with a beauty of its own, so distinct from chess itself that many of the most enthusiastic problemists rarely play an ordinary game. The majority of chess-players, however, take a friendly interest in problems.

In each of the positions illustrated there is one move possible for White, by making which he can force mate, in the stipulated number of moves, against any defence by Black whatsoever. The move is the 'key-move' or solution to the problem.

The art of chess problems consists in making this key-move the most unlikely looking move in the position, or introducing beautiful or subtle play, Black making clever attempts at defence which White brilliantly frustrates.

Don't tackle any 'mate in three' problem until you have solved 20 or 30 two-movers; a good three-mover may take even an expert an hour or more to solve. Don't look up a solution until you are pretty certain you have allowed for every possible reply by Black, including checks to the White king, pinning of one or more white pieces, etc. If your solution is wrong, search even more carefully for the defensive resource you have overlooked. It helps to put the problem away if it troubles you overmuch, and sleep on it. When you return to it, your mind will be fresh and you will notice things overlooked before. When you have solved three or four problems *unaided*, your knowledge of chess and chess problems will advance by leaps and bounds.

PROBLEM No. 5
By COMINS MANSFIELD

BLACK

Figure 39

White to play and mate in two moves

PROBLEM No. 6 By A. G. STUBBS

BLACK

Figure 40

White to play and mate in two moves

PROBLEM No. 7 By F. FLYNN
(The Sign of the Cross)

BLACK

Figure 41

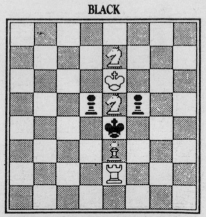

White to play and mate in two moves

PROBLEM No. 8 By C. CHRISTENSEN

BLACK

Figure 42

White to play and mate in two moves

PROBLEM No. 9 By B. G. LAWS, London

BLACK

Figure 43

White to play and mate in two moves

121

PROBLEM No. 10 ANONYMOUS

BLACK

Figure 44

White to play and mate in two moves

Solutions to Chess Problems

Problem No. 1. White — Rook to King's Bishop's 8th, or K N 8 or K R 8. Black — King takes Knight. White — King to Queen's 7th — mate.

NB. This problem was composed to illustrate the dangers of stalemate; for instance, if White makes any move with his King, Black immediately obtains a draw by stalemate.

Problem No. 2. White — Pawn to Queen's Bishop's 5th. Black – Pawn to Queen's 4th. White — Takes Pawn *en passant*. Black — Any. White – Knight to Queen's Bishop's 4th — mate.

NB. This position was composed to illustrate the *en passant* move of the Pawn.

Problem No. 3. White — Pawn to Queen's Knight's 8th (becomes a Knight). Black — Any. White — Knight to King's 4th — mate. This position was composed with the object of demonstrating to the novice the fact that in 'queening' a pawn it may at times best serve the real object of his game (checkmate) to choose an inferior rather than a superior piece.

Problem No. 4. White — Pawn to Queen's 4th (discovers check). Black — King takes Knight. White — Castles, mate. This position was composed with the object of forcibly impressing upon the novice the power of the Pawn to move two squares on its initial play; of the King to Castle, should the condition of the game make such a move desirable; and to illustrate the offensive power of *each* piece — excepting the absent Queen — in attack on the opposing King.

No. 5. By Comins Mansfield. White — Knight to Queen's 7th. Black — Any. White mates accordingly.

No. 6. By A. G. Stubbs. White — Queen to Bishop's 7th. Black — Any. White mates accordingly.

No. 7. By F. Flynn. White — Knight to Queen's 5th. Black — Pawn to King's Bishop's 5th. White — Knight to Queen's Bishop's 3rd, mate.

No. 8. By C. Christensen. White — Queen to Bishop's 8th. Black — Any. White mates accordingly.

No. 9. By B. G. Laws. White — Queen to Rook's 8th. Black — Any. White mates accordingly.

No. 10. Anonymous. White — Rook to Bishop's 3rd. Black — Any. White mates accordingly.

Chapter 12

INSTRUCTIVE GAMES

◼▬▬▬▬▬   ▬▬▬▬◻

T he purpose of this chapter is to study the complete game as an organic process. Here we see the opening moves and appraise their likely consequences. We see the early jockeying for advantage, and we are able to judge whether these attempts will succeed or fail. We see the coming of the crisis, when respective resources will either triumph or shrivel. Each game is a kind of sermon which preaches the virtues of effective development and denounces the defects of bad development. The games are extracted from *Beginner's Guide To Winning Chess* by Fred Reinfeld (W. Foulsham & Co., 1991) which is a recommended title for those students wishing to obtain further reading. Remember that in the notation '?' is used to denote 'good move', while '!' is used for the opposite.

Centre Game (Leipzig, 1903)

	WHITE	BLACK
	Amateur	*Leonhardt*
1	P — K 4	P — K 4
2	P — Q 4	. . . .

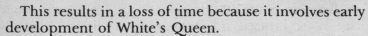
This results in a loss of time because it involves early development of White's Queen.

2	. . . .	P × P
3	Q × P	N — Q B 3

Black gains time by attacking the White Queen.

4	Q — K 3	N — B 3

Black has achieved a substantial lead in development.

5	B — B 4	. . . .

White would do better to develop his Queen-side pieces and castle on that wing.

5	. . . .	N — K 4

Black has just moved his Queen Knight a second time. Generally we would dismiss this as faulty opening play.

BLACK

Figure 45

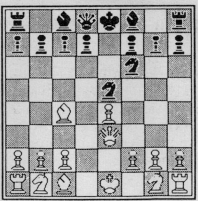

White to move

After 5 . . . . N — K 4

However, since White has lost time previously, Black can allow himself this luxury. In addition, Black is attacking White's Bishop, which further minimizes the loss of time involved in the Knight move.

6   B — N 3   . . . .

It would have been safer to retreat 6 B — K 2, but this would have underlined the pointlessness of White's previous move.

6   . . . .   B — N 5 ch.

This crafty move is best answered by development, say 7 N — Q B 3 or 7 B — Q 2, after which White would be on the way to closing up the gap in development.

7   P — Q B 3   . . . .

But this mechanical reply does not help White's development and, in fact, invites trouble.

7   . . . .   B — B 4!

This tricky move invites 8 Q × B? which would cost White his Queen. The same is true of 8 Q — B 4?

White's safest retreat would have been 8 Q — K 2. But even this comparatively safe move might be objected to, because it would mean that White would have to move his Queen three times to reach a square which originally could have been reached in one move. In any event, Black would still have maintained a commanding lead in development.

8   Q — N 3??   . . . .

In making this attractive move, White is under the mistaken impression that he is gaining time by attacking the advanced Black Knight.

9 . . . .   B × P ch!!
   Resigns

A surprise finish. The point is that the Bishop check attacks White's King and Queen; hence, the Bishop must be captured. However, either way of capturing exposes White to a Knight forcing check which forces

BLACK *to move*

Figure 46

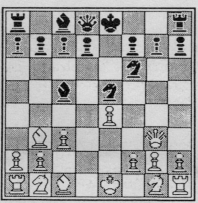

WHITE

After 8 Q — N 3??

the win of White's Queen. Consequently, White surrenders with what at first seems surprising suddenness.

A dramatic lesson on the consequences of dawdling development.

Giuoco Piano (Berlin, 1907)

	WHITE	BLACK
	Scheve	*Teichmann*
1	P — K 4	P — K 4
2	N — K B 3	N — Q B 3
3	B — B 4	B — B 4
4	P — B 3	. . . .

Here White proposes to set up a broad Pawn centre with P — Q 4.

4	. . . .	Q — K 2

In the event of P — Q 4, Black has no intention of replying . . . P × P, for then White would obtain a very powerful game with P × P. Instead, Black intends to answer P — Q 4 with . . . B — N 3, maintaining his hold on the centre.

BLACK

Figure 47

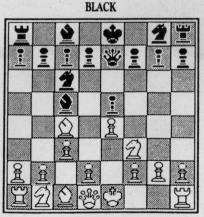

White to move

After 4 . . . . Q — K 2

5	Castles	P — Q 3

And now Black is quite content with the possibility of 6 P — Q 4, B — N 3; 7 P × P, P × P by which he maintains a firm hold on the centre.

6	P — Q 4	B — N 3
7	P — Q R 4	. . . .

Very tricky. White threatens 8 P — R 5, B × R P?; 9 P — Q 5 winning a piece. There is also another threat: 8 P — R 5, N × R P, 9 R × N, B × R; 10 Q — R ch by which White wins the loose Bishop and remains ahead in material with two minor pieces for a Rook and Pawn.

7	. . . .	P — Q R 3

Black parries the threat.

8	P — R 5	B — R 2

After 8 . . . N × R P; 9 R × N, B × R; 10 Q — R 4 ch, P — Q N 4; 11 Q × B, P × B; 12 Q — R 4 ch followed by Q × B P; White has two Pawns for the Exchange, and the outcome is unclear.

9	P — R 3	. . . .

This move has good and bad features. White prevents the annoying pin . . . B — N 5, but he creates a weakness in his castled position which can prove very costly under certain conditions.

9	. . . .	N — B 3

White should now play 10 R — K 1 — or even 10 P — Q 5 if he is unwilling to maintain the broad Pawn centre.

BLACK

Figure 48

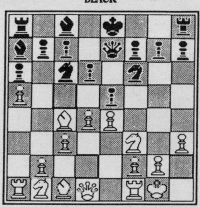

White to move

After 9 . . . . N — B 3

10   P × P?   . . . .

Feeble and spineless. Black's pieces suddenly come to life, particularly his Bishop tucked away at Queen Rook 2. This Bishop acquires a magnificently elongated diagonal reaching right down to White King's territory.

10   . . . .   Q N × P

Now this Knight is in good play too. Perhaps White's best reply was 11 B — K 2, although the protection of his King Pawn would soon begin to present problems. The initiative has definitely passed to Black.

11   N × N   . . . .

After this feeble move White is really in trouble.

11   . . . .   Q × N !

131

Now Black's Queen is powerfully in play. It is true that 12 Q — B 3 would prevent Black's next move, but then Black could simply play 12 . . . Q × K P; 13 Q × Q, N × Q; as the pinning move 14 R — K 1 would lose for White.

12   N — Q 2   . . . .

BLACK *to move*

Figure 49

WHITE

After 12 N — Q 2

White protects his King Pawn, but he fails to see Black's other threat.

12   . . . .   B × R P !

Now the weakening of White's castled position comes to light.

132

White's situation has become very trying. If he plays
13 N — B 3, Black wins with 13 . . . Q — N 6 (threatens
. . . Q × N P mate while White's King Bishop Pawn is
pinned, so that 14 P × Q is out of the question);
14 N — K 1, N — N 5.

Another possibility is 13 Q — B 3, B — N 5; 14 Q —
Q 3, Castles/K; and Black is a Pawn ahead with a
fine game.

13	P × B	. . . .

After this White is definitely lost, since his castled
position is open to the enemy.

13	. . . .	Q — N 6 ch.

The point: White's pinned King Bishop Pawn cannot
capture the Queen.

14	K — R 1	Q × R P ch.
15	K — N 1	N — N 5

Threatening mate.

16	N — B 3	Q — N 6 ch.

See the note to Black's thirteenth move.

17	K — R 1	B × P

White resigns, as he has no good defence against the
threat of 18 . . . Q — R 6 ch and mate next move. After
18 B — B 4, Q × B, White would be defenceless against
the coming 19 . . . Q — N 6.

The combination of 10 P × P? and 13 P × B proved
fatal for White. The first of these moves opened up the
terrible diagonal for Black's King Bishop; the second
left White's castled position exposed to crushing attack.

BLACK

Figure 50

White to move

After 17 . . . . B × P

Ruy Lopez (Match, 1893)

	WHITE	BLACK
	Tarrasch	*Tchigorin*
1	P — K 4	P — K 4
2	N — K B 3	N — Q B 3
3	B — N 5	P — Q R 3
4	B — R 4	N — B 3
5	N — B 3	. . . .

In modern play the alternative 5 Castles is customary.

5	. . . .	B — N 5

This is out of place here; Black should play
5 . . . B — K 2.

134

6 N — Q 5 !   . . . .

A difficult move to answer effectively. For example, if
6 . . . N × N; 7 P × N, N — K 2; 8 N × P, N × P;
9 B — N 3; and Black is in trouble.

6 . . . .   B — R 4 ?

After this the Bishop is out of play for the rest of the
game. The right move was 6 . . . B — K 2.

7	Castles	P — Q N 4
8	B — N 3	P — Q 3
9	P — Q 3	B — K N 5

Figure 51

BLACK

White to move

After 9 . . . B — K N 5

Having pinned White's King Knight, Black is now
ready to play . . . N — Q 5 in order to break up the

Pawns in front of White's castled position. To prevent this, White plays:

    10 P — B 3   . . . .

Black would like to castle, but then comes 11 B — N 5 forcing the break-up of Black's King-side Pawns.

Black's safest course was doubtless 10 . . . P — R 3 (preventing B — N 5) followed by castling.

    10 . . . .   N — K 2 ??

Black sees that after 10 . . . N × N; 11 B × N, Q — Q 2; 12 B × N, Q × B; 13 N × P !, B × Q; 14 N × Q; White would win material because both Black Bishops would be under attack. (Note how the unfortunate position of Black's Bishop on Queen Rook 4 continues to cause trouble!)

However, the plausible move actually played by Black is also a dangerous one.

BLACK

Figure 52

White to move

After 10 . . . N — K 2 ??

11   N × K P !!   . . . .

An astonishing offer of the Queen. The point is that
after 11 ... B × Q; 12 N × N ch, P × N??; there
follows 13 B × P ch, K — B 1; 14 B — R 6 mate.

11   . . . .   P × N

To be sure, Black can put up a more stubborn defence
with 11 ... B × Q; 12 N × N ch, K — B 1; 13 N/K 5 —
Q 7 ch, Q × N; 14 N × Q ch, K — K 1; 15 R × B,
K × N. However, with a Pawn down Black would be
certain to lose the ensuing endgame.

12   N × N ch   . . . .

By capturing this Knight with check, White gains the
time to capture the Black Bishop.

12   . . . .   P × N
13   Q × B   . . . .

Thus, White remains a Pawn ahead, as 13 ...
Q × P?? would be ruinous for Black.

Note that Black cannot castle. It will soon become
apparent that his King is exposed to a dangerous
attack.

13   . . . .   N — N 3
14   B — Q 5   Q R — N 1
15   P — K B 4 !   . . . .

If Black castles now, he loses a piece. With his King
forced to remain in the centre, he will soon be exposed
to a withering attack along the King Bishop file.

15   . . . .   P — B 3

■ □

BLACK *to move*

Figure 53

WHITE

After 15 P — K B 4 !

Black gives away a second Pawn, hoping for complications.

16	B × Q B P ch	K — K 2

And now of course Black can never castle. At the moment he threatens ... Q — N 3 ch with a double attack which would win White's advanced Bishop. Naturally White avoids this possibility.

17	B — Q 5	P — N 5
18	P × K P	Q — N 3 ch
19	K — R 1	N × P
20	Q — R 5	. . . .

White is getting to work in earnest. He threatens 21 R × P!! (note the good work along the open King

Bishop file), so that if 21 ... K × R; then 22 Q — N 5 mate — or 21 ... Q × R; then 22 B — N 5, winning Black's Queen.

20 . . . .   N — N 3

BLACK *to move*

Figure 54

WHITE

After 20 N — N 3

21   R × P !!   . . . .

This still works, thanks to the exposed state of Black's King and the disorganized state of his other forces.

21   . . . .   K × R

What now follows is a classic example of concentrated attack against a helpless King.

| 22 | B — N 5 ch. | K — N 2 |

The alternative 22 ... K — K 4 lets White mate in two moves.

| 23 | Q — R 6 ch. | K — N 1 |
| 24 | R — K B 1 | . . . . |

Triumph of the open King Bishop file. White threatens mate on the move.

| 24 | . . . . | R — K B 1 |
| 25 | B — K B 6 | . . . . |

Once more White threatens mate on the move.

| 25 | . . . . | Q × B |

BLACK *to move*

Figure 55

WHITE

After 26 R × Q

The only defence for the moment.

| 26 | R × Q | Resigns |

Black realises that he is defenceless against the threat of 27 R × N ch !, R P × N; 28 Q × P mate.

Note that Black's misplaced Bishop remained useless to the very end of the game.

Queen Fianchetto Defence
(Philadelphia, 1859) [White plays blindfold]

	WHITE	BLACK
	Morphy	*Lewis*
1	P — K 4	P — Q N 3

This is our first game in which Black refuses to answer 1 P — K 4 with 1 . . . P — K 4. The move he has selected is too passive, because it gives White a completely free hand in the centre.

| 2 | P — Q 4 | . . . . |

White immediately forms a broad Pawn centre.

2	. . . .	B — N 2
3	B — Q 3	P — K 3
4	N — K R 3 !	. . . .

An unusual and highly interesting move. Morphy was of course well aware that a Knight is generally poorly placed at the side of the board. His object here was to make room for the advance of his King Bishop Pawn. (This would be ruled out by the more orthodox 4 N — K B 3.)

As for the Knight at the side of the board, White foresees a brilliant future for him.

| 4 | . . . . | P — Q 4 |

Rather late in the day Black decides to make a stand in the centre. However, this turns out badly.

| 5 | P — K 5 ! | . . . . |

BLACK *to move*

Figure 56

WHITE

After 5 P — K 5 !

White has a distinct advantage. Black's Queen Bishop has no scope and his King-side pieces have miserable prospects. White's Pawn wedge at King 5 heralds a King-side attack — if only because this Pawn prevents Black from developing his King Knight to King Bishop 3, the most effective defensive post for this Knight.

    5 . . . .   N — K 2

Note by the way that while Black's fianchettoed Bishop at Queen Knight 2 is shut out of the game, White's Bishop at Queen 3 has a magnificent diagonal.

    6 Castles   N — N 3
    7 P — K B 4 !   . . . .

Very well played. White intends to push the Pawn ahead, opening the King Bishop file for attacking pur-

poses. In doing so, he is carrying out the underlying
idea behind 4 N — K R 3 !

7	. . . .	B — K 2
8	P — B 5 !	P × P
9	B × P	B — B 1

Not a bad idea. Since this Bishop is destined to be
useless, Black exchanges him for White's valuable
Bishop. Unfortunately, this sensible manoeuvre does
not prove too helpful, because White's lead in development and mobility still remains substantial.

| 10 | B × B | Q × B |
| 11 | N — B 3 | . . . . |

Morphy's speciality: developing and gaining time.

11	. . . .	P — Q B 3
12	B — N 5 !	Castles
13	B × B	N × B

BLACK

Figure 57

WHITE *to move*

After 13 . . . N × B

143

14   Q — R 5 !   . . . .

White has formidable attacking prospects based on the aggressive position of his Queen and his control of the open King Bishop file.

White now threatens to win at least a Pawn by 15 N — K N 5 (threatening mate), P — K R 3; 16 N × B P, etc.

Black loses quickly after 14 . . . P — N 3; 15 Q — R 6, N — B 4; 16 R × N !, Q × R; 17 N — K N 5, R — K 1; 18 R — K B 1, etc.

Also if 14 . . . Q — K 3; 15 R — B 3 !, N — Q 2; 16 Q R — K B 1; the pressure on the King Bishop file must be decisive. If Black tries to neutralize it with 16 . . . P — B 3, then 17 N — B 4 ! wins — for example, 17 . . . Q — B 4; 18 Q × Q, N × Q; 19 N — K 6, etc; or 17 . . . Q — B 2; 18 Q × Q ch, etc.

14   . . . .   P — K R 3

Black prevents N — K N 5, but at the cost of weakening his castled position. The ensuing play is a good example of how one can take advantage of such a weakening.

15   R — B 3 !   . . . .

White prepares to double Rooks on the King Bishop file, and he also contemplates R — N 3 threatening Q × R P and, thus, exploiting the weakness created by 14 . . . P — K R 3.

15   . . . .   N — N 3

This is intended to neutralize some of White's pressure on the King Bishop and King Knight files.

16 Q R — K B 1 !   Q — K 3

Both players have made their dispositions for the coming phase. White has the upper hand because both of his Rooks are in the fray while Black has only one Rook doing defensive work.

BLACK

Figure 58

WHITE *to move.*

After 16 Q — K 3

17 N — K 2 !   . . . .

White proceeds to remove Black's defensive Knight in order to increase his overwhelming superiority on the King-side.

17	. . . .	N — Q 2
18	N/K 2 — B 4 !	N × N
19	N × N	Q — K 2
20	R — K N 3	. . . .

White threatens 21 Q × R P. Now that Black's protective Knight has disappeared, his King-side must collapse under the pressure.

$$12 \quad \dots \quad\quad\quad\quad K - R 2$$

This parries the threat, but there will be new ones.

$$21 \quad R/B 1 - B 3 ! \quad\quad\quad\quad \dots$$

This renews the pressure with a vengeance.

White now threatens 22 R × P ch!, K × R; 23 R — K N 3 ch. Thus if 23 . . . K — R 2; 24 R — K R 3 wins, as 24 . . . Q — N 4 is useless.

Again, if 23 . . . Q — N 4; then 24 R × Q ch, P × R; 25 Q × N P ch. Now further Queen checks will win Black's Knight, leaving White with a comfortable advantage in material.

BLACK

Figure 59

WHITE *to move*

After 21 R/B 1 — B 3 !

Black cannot defend himself with 21 . . . P — N 3, for then White wins with 22 N × N P, P × N; 23 R × P, etc.

| 21 | . . . . | R — K N 1 |
| 22 | N — R 3 ! | . . . . |

White's main threat is now 23 N — N 5 ch, K — R 1; 24 N × P ch, K — R 2; 25 Q — N 6 mate.

| 22 | . . . . | P — N 3 |
| 23 | N — N 5 ch! | . . . . |

This leaves Black no choice, for after 23 . . . K — N 2; 24 R × P ch, Q × R; 25 N × Q; Black is unable to play 25 . . . P × Q.

| 23 | . . . . | Q × N |
| 24 | R × P ch. | . . . . |

And now if 24 . . . R — N 2; 25 R × R ch, K × R; 26 R × Q; Black cannot play 26 . . . P × Q. If he plays 26 . . . P × R; White replies 27 Q × P/N 5 with an easy win.

| 24 | . . . . | K — R 1 |

Now White can win easily with 25 R × Q, P × Q; 26 R × R ch followed by 27 R × N. But he does much better.

| 25 | Q × Q ! | Resigns |

For if 25 . . . P × Q; 26 R — K R 3 mate. The faultless and efficient manner in which White carried out the attack is beyond all praise.

BLACK *to move*

Figure 60

WHITE

After 25 Q × Q !

Sicilian Defence
(National Intercollegiate Championship, 1929)

WHITE	BLACK
Reinfeld	*Grossman*
1 P — K 4	P — Q B 4

Here too Black avoids playing 1 . . . P — K 4. But at least 1 . . . P — Q B 4 makes more sense than 1 . . . P — Q N 3, for the advance of Black's Queen Bishop Pawn restrains White from forming a broad Pawn centre with P — Q 4.

2 N — K B 3	N — Q B 3
3 P — Q 4	. . . .

148

Since the threatened P — Q 5 would stifle Black's game, he naturally exchanges Pawns.

3	. . . .	P × P
4	N × P	. . . .

As a result of the exchange of Pawns, White has a half-open Queen file while Black has a half-open Queen Bishop file. Each player hopes to put the half-open file to good use.

4	. . . .	N — B 3
5	N — Q B 3	P — Q 3
6	B — K 2	P — Q R 3

Black wants to play . . . Q — B 2 without having his Queen disturbed by N — N 5.

7	Castles	Q — B 2

It would have been safer to play . . . P — K 3 in order to prevent White's next move. Instead, Black deliberately courts this move in order to win a Pawn.

8	N — Q 5 !	K N × N
9	P × N	N × N
10	Q × N	Q × P ?

Black has lost valuable time and soon finds himself considerably behind in development.

11	B — Q B 4	Q — N 3

Black loses more time with the Queen, but he has little choice. His prime difficulty is that he cannot develop his King Bishop; this makes it impossible for him to castle and leaves his King vulnerable to attack.

12	B — B 4	Q — B 3
13	Q — K 3	. . . .

BLACK

Figure 61

WHITE *to move*

After 10 Q × P

It is clearly in White's interest to avoid the exchange of Queens. Black might now try 13 ... P — R 3; 14 K R — K 1, P — K N 4 (if 14 ... Q × P; 15 B × Q P); 15 B — K N 3, B — N 2; but after 16 Q — N 6, Castles; 17 Q — B 7; White has all the play.

13	. . . .	P — K 4
14	P × P e.p.!	. . . .

Very important. If White is to make his advantage in mobility tell, he must open new lines.

14	. . . .	B × P
15	K R — K 1	K — Q 2
16	B — K N 5 !	Q — B 4
17	Q — N 6 !	. . . .

BLACK *to move*

Figure 62

WHITE

After 17 Q — N 6 !

White's offer of both Bishops comes as a stunning surprise, but it is actually grounded on strict logic.

If Black plays 17 ... B × B, White replies 18 Q × N P mate.

If Black plays 17 ... Q × B, White replies 18 Q × N P ch and then captures Black's Rook with check.

17	. . . .	R — B 1

Black does no better with 17 ... Q R — N 1 in view of 18 B × B ch, P × B; 19 Q R — B 1 with the irresistible threat of 20 Q — B 7 ch.

The fact is that the dangerous position of Black's King in the centre exposes him to one vicious threat after another.

| 18 | B × B ch | P × B |
| 19 | Q R — B 1 | . . . . |

White can afford to ignore the attack on his Bishop as he threatens 20 Q × N P ch followed by 21 R × R mate.

| 19 | . . . . | Q — N 4 |

This is the only defence, but White has a powerful reply.

| 19 | Q — K 3 ! | . . . . |

BLACK *to move*

Figure 63

WHITE

After 20 Q — K 3 !

Threatening 21 Q × P mate.

152

Note that 20 ... P — K 4 cannot be played, as it would lead to 21 Q — K R 3 ch, K — K 1; 22 Q — K 6 ch and mate next move.

Or 20 ... Q — K B 4; 21 R × R, K × R; 22 R — Q B 1 ch, K — N 1; 23 B — Q 8 ! and Black is lost.

| 20 | .... | R — K 1 |

He parries the mate threat but in so doing he surrenders the Queen Bishop file.

| 21 | R — B 3 ! | .... |

White intends to play 22 K R — Q B 1 with the terrible threat of R — B 7 mate.

| 21 | .... | P — Q 4 |

Now Black can answer 22 K R — Q B 1 with 22 ... B — Q 3. So White selects a different way, involving magnificent *centralising* of his Queen.

| 22 | Q — K 5 | .... |

With a double mate threat.

| 22 | .... | Q — N 3 |

Or 22 ... B — Q 3; 23 Q × N P ch, B — K 2; 24 B × B, K R — N 1; 25 Q — B 7 and wins, as 25 ... R × B is answered by 26 Q × R/N 8.

| 23 | K R — Q B 1 | Resigns |

Black is helpless against the threat of 24 R — B 7 ch followed by mate next move. If Black tries 23 ... B — Q 3, then 24 Q × N P ch, B — K 2; 25 B × B is crushing.

BLACK *to move*

Figure 64

WHITE

After 23 K R — Q B 1

A very instructive game because of White's skill in using the open lines against Black's hapless King. Note that it was Black's ill-judged 10 . . . Q × P ? that opened the Queen Bishop file for White.

NOTES

NOTES

NOTES